P-51 Mustang

DAVID OLIVER

AMBERLEY

Acknowledgements

Of the many who have provided a stream of information and images, I would like to thank to following individuals, organisations and archives: Les Billcliff, James Craik, Lynn Garrison, Geoff Goodall, A. L. Homersham, Bruce Potts, Francois Prins, Edward Richie, John Trathome, BravoBravo Aviation, Forgotten Props, Swiss Mustangs, World War Photos, WW2DB, Norfolk Record Office (NRO), North American Aviation (NAA), US National Archives (NA), US Library of Congress (LOC), National Aeronautics and Space Administration (NASA), Imperial War Museum (IWM), San Diego Air and Space Museum, United Nations (UN), and US National Air and Space Museum (NASM).

First published 2023

Amberley Publishing
The Hill, Stroud,
Gloucestershire, GL5 4EP

www.amberley-books.com

ISBN 978 1 3981 1055 7 (print)
ISBN 978 1 3981 1056 4 (ebook)

British Library Cataloguing in Publication Data.
A catalogue record for this book is available from the British Library.

Typeset in 11pt on 14pt Celeste.
Typesetting by SJmagic DESIGN SERVICES, India.
Printed in the UK.

Contents

Introduction

The North American P-51 Mustang was undoubtedly one of the most versatile and successful piston-engined single-seat fighters of the Second World War. Originally designed to meet a British requirement, early versions quickly demonstrated their superior performance over contemporary fighter aircraft and when later Mustangs were fitted with a Rolls-Royce Merlin engine the Allies had one of the truly great fighters of the twentieth century.

The fitting of drop tanks allowed Mustangs to escort American bombers all the way to Berlin and back, which were then dubbed 'Little friends'. The everyday appearance of such a superb Allied fighter over the German capital sounded the death knell of the Third Reich. Apart from being the most successful aircraft of its type, the Mustang illustrates the close co-operation between the USA and the UK. The Americans produced one of the best fighter airframes in the world and when matched to the superb British Rolls-Royce Merlin aero-engine a thoroughbred was born.

The P-51 Mustang was one of the few fighter aircraft that fought in the Second World War to be designed after that conflict began. It was a private venture by a company that was less than a decade old, and was able to complete its design with incredible speed for a foreign customer. When it was given the British engine and an even greater fuel capacity, the P-51 flew missions far longer than any fighter aircraft had ever flown.

The P-51 flew for the first time on 25 October 1940, and it remained in service with the Allied air forces during the Korean War and for foreign military air arms well into the 1980s.

A total of 14,819 Mustangs of all types were built in the United States during the Second World War. The Mustang created records from the day of its inspired conception, and the rapid development processes through which it passed were phenomenal by any standard and ended the war as the best all-round fighter used by any of the combatants.

CHAPTER ONE

Development and Production

What would be the most successful piston-engined single-seat fighter aircraft produced by any nation during the Second World War, the P-51 Mustang owed its origin to the British Air Purchasing Commission. In April 1940, it asked North American Aviation to manufacture the Hawk 87A-1 under license from Curtiss-Wright for the Royal Air Force (RAF).

Despite never having produced a fighter aircraft, North American's president, James H. 'Dutch' Kindelberger, maintained that his company could produce an entirely new fighter, which, designed around the same 1,200-hp Allison V-1710-39 engine that powered the Hawk, would be superior on all counts to the Curtiss fighter. The broad outline of the new fighter had already been conceived as a result of air combat reports from the war in Europe, and the Commission agreed to the proposal on the understanding that the aircraft met its requirements and stipulated that in view of the serious war situation faced by the RAF, that a prototype be completed within 120 days.

The prototype, designated the NA-73X, was designed by a team headed by Raymond Rice and German-born Edgar Schmued, who had worked for the Fokker Aircraft Corporation of America in the 1930s, which was owned by General Motors. When General Motors sold its air arm it became the forerunner of North American Aviation, which Schmued joined in 1936.

The NA-73X was rolled out in 117 days, although it lacked the Allison engine. This delayed the first flight until Vance Breese flew on 26 October 1940, by which time the first British contract for 320 aircraft had been placed at a price of $37,590 per aircraft, while two aircraft from the initial production batch would be transferred to the US Army Air Corps (USAAC) for evaluation.

One of the first fighter aircraft designs to employ a laminar-flow wing, the sleek all-metal stressed-skin NA-73X had a trouble-free flight test flight programme and production started at the beginning of 1941 at a rate of fifty a month. The second production aircraft arrived in the United Kingdom in October 1941, named the Mustang I.

The new aircraft was immediately recognised as being superior in every way to previous American fighters, although handicapped by the low-rated altitude of its Allison engine, which prevented its use for normal fighter duties. However, its impressive low-altitude performance and maneuverability, and heavy armament comprising two 0.5-inch MG 53 Browning machine guns mounted in the nose and below the engine, plus one 0.5-inch and two 0.3-inch MG 40 guns in each wing, made it ideal for the tactical reconnaissance and ground attack roles.

The first RAF NA-83 Mustang, AG345, was tested in America by the BPC while AG346 was shipped to Britain in November 1941. The third aircraft, AG365, was tested by pilots of the Aeroplane and Armament Experimental Establishment at Boscombe Down and the Air Fighting Development Unit at Duxford for tactical evaluation. They found it possessed excellent qualities as a low- and medium-altitude fighter.

On 29 December 1941 the first XP-51 fighter prototype, 73-3101, arrived at the National Advisory Committee for Aeronautics Langley Memorial Aeronautical Laboratory at Langley Field, Virginia, and at Wright Field, Ohio, for evaluation. This was the fourth production RAF Mustang I, RAF serial AG348. The XP-51 found favour with its test pilots but the Air Material Command placed no orders on behalf of the USAAC.

Shortly after the first Mustang I was delivered to Liverpool on 24 October 1941, consideration was given to the cross-breeding of North American Aviation's airframe with the British Rolls-Royce Merlin 61 engine to improve the fighter's high-altitude performance, a development that would be destined to create the pre-eminent all-round fighter aircraft of the Second World War. One man who had a great influence over the development of the P-51 Mustang was Lt Col Thomas J. Hitchcock Jr, who at seventeen began his military career during the First World War with the French Lafayette Flying Corps after being turned away by the US Army for being too young. Earning his wings with the French, Hitchcock scored three aerial victories before being shot down and captured. After being held captive for six months, he jumped from a moving train and walked more than 100 miles to the safety of Switzerland.

After the war, Hitchcock became an accomplished polo player, worked as an investment banker, and lived the life of a socialite. When the United States entered the Second World War, Hitchcock secured a commission in the US Army Air Force (USAAF) hoping to command a fighter squadron. At forty-two, however, he was considered too old for combat.

After his appointment as Assistant Military Air Attaché in London, Hitchcock reported to Washington on the results of British tests involving the Mustang I and the Rolls-Royce Merlin 61 engine.

Four Mustang Is were delivered to Rolls-Royce at Hucknall, known as Mustang Xs, fitted with the Merlin 61 or Merlin 65 driving four-bladed airscrews to absorb the extra power. Flown by Roll-Royce test pilot Ronald Hawker from April

1942, the results were nothing short of astounding. The Merlin engine-powered Mustangs reached speeds in excess of 430 miles per hour at 30,000 feet, almost 100 miles per hour faster than the Allison engine.

Unsurprisingly, Hitchcock's report to Washington at the end of 1942 recommended immediate development of the NA-99 P-51A into a high-altitude fighter by replacing the Allison engine with the Merlin, which was already being produced for the British in the United States under license by the Packard Motor Company. The North American company began adapting two airframes to take the US-built Packard Merlin V-1650-3 engine as NA-101 XP-51Bs and flight tests began in September 1942. Equipped with a deepened ventral radiator and new ailerons, the XP-51B was found to be capable of a maximum speed of 441 mph at 29,800 feet, and it climbed to 20,000 feet in 5.9 minutes. The USAAF placed an immediate order for 2,200 of the new NA-101 P-51Bs and by the summer of 1943 the Merlin-engined Mustangs were in full-scale production at Inglewood in California and at a new plant in Dallas, Texas.

Between 1942 and 1943, 1,988 P-51Bs and 1,750 P-51Cs were built armed with four or six 0.5-inch machine guns in the wings. The last 550 P-51Bs had the addition of an 85 US gallon fuselage fuel tank, giving them a range of 1,300 miles. Some 250 P-51Bs and 637 P-51Cs were supplied to the RAF under the Lend-Lease agreement as Mustang IIIs.

The concern expressed by the RAF about the Mustang's rearward view led to the decision in 1944 to introduce a major redesign in order to fit a streamlined 'bubble' canopy on a cut-down rear fuselage to what was to become the most widely produced variant of the Mustang, the P-51D, 7,956 of which were built. On 17 November 1943 a modified P-51B reconfigured as the NA-106 XP-51D made its first flight at Inglewood. As production got into its stride a dorsal fin was introduced to compensate for the loss of keel surface on the rear fuselage.

Powered by the Packard-built Rolls-Royce Merlin V-1650-7 engine rated at 1,450 hp for take-off and 1,695 hp under war emergency conditions at 10,300 feet, the NA-109 P-51D attained a maximum speed of 395 mph at 5,000 feet, 413 mph at 15,000 feet and 437 mph at 25,000 feet. Its absolute range was no less than 2,080 miles and it had an endurance of 8 hours 20 minutes.

Armed with six 0.5-inch Colt-Browning machine guns, it could also carry two 1,000-lb bombs, ten 5-inch-high velocity rockets or a cluster of Bazooka-type rocket-launching tubes under each wing.

For the tactical reconnaissance role, 136 P-51Ds were fitted with oblique and vertical cameras in the rear fuselage and received the designation F-6D. Ten were fitted with an extra seat with full dual controls for use as conversion trainers and high speed liaison aircraft under the designation TP-51D.

As Deputy Chief of Staff of the 9th Air Support Command in charge of tactical research and development of the Mustang programme, Hitchcock insisted on pinpointing any problems himself rather than risking the lives of his men. He was unable to pull his Mustang out of a dive during a test flight on 18 April 1944 and died in the subsequent crash near Salisbury, England.

The final production of the Mustang was the NA-126 P-51H, which embodied experience gained from the experimental lightweight NA-105 XP-51F and XP-51G Mustangs flown in 1944. Powered by a 2,218-hp Packard V-1650-9 Merlin, the P-51H attained a top speed of 487 mph at 25,000 feet, making it the fastest Mustang to see service. The first P-51H flew on 3 February 1945 followed by 554 production aircraft that were too late to take part in operations over Europe, although it had begun to equip a number of fighter groups when the war with Japan ended. VJ Day resulted in the cancellation of 1,445 P-51H and 1,700 P-51L Mustangs with the more powerful V-1650-11 engine.

Left: The first production RAF Mustang I AG345 was retained by North American for flight development. (NAA)

Below: The second North American NA-73 designated XP-51, serial number 41-039, was evaluated by the USAAC at Langley Field in 1941. (NASA)

The Mustang all-metal stressed skin fuselage production line at the North American facility at Inglewood, California, in 1942. (LOC)

The NA-97 A-36A Apache production line at Inglewood, California, in 1942. (NARA)

A tail fin of the all-metal A-36A Apache being worked on by a North American worker at Inglewood. (NA)

The basic instrument panel in the A-36A Apache's cockpit. (USAF)

Cannon-armed NA-91 P-51A 41-137416 on a test flight over California in October 1942 was delivered to the RAF as a Mustang 1A. (LOC)

One of two NA-101 XP-51Bs, 41-37352, fitted with the US-built Packard Merlin V-1650-3 engine and flight tested in September 1942. (NAA)

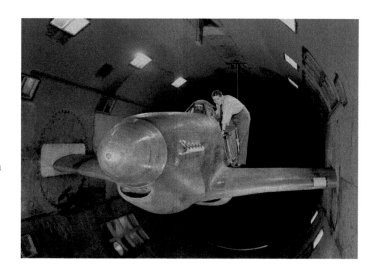

North American Aviation P-51B in the full-scale wind tunnel at NACA Langley Memorial Aeronautical Laboratory, Hampton, Virginia, in September 1943. (NASA)

Early production NA-102 P-51B-1-NA 43-12342 prepares for the test flight at Inglewood. (NAA)

Robert Chilton, North American test pilot, about to test P-51B-19-NA 41-106435 at Inglewood. (NAA)

RAF Mustang I AL975 fitted with a Merlin 61 at Rolls-Royce at Hucknall, tested by Ron Harker, known as a Mustang X. (RAF)

RAF Mustang II FR917 being wrapped in plastic at Inglewood and crated for shipment to Britain. (NAA)

A USAAF P-51C-1-NT assigned to the Army Tactical Center at Orlando in Florida in 1943. (USAF)

Above: USAAF
P-51C-10-NT 43-24943 built
at Dallas, Texas, in 1944.
(NAA).

Right: Wind tunnel tests
of a model fitted with a
bubble canopy revealed
smooth airflow over the
modified surfaces. (NAA)

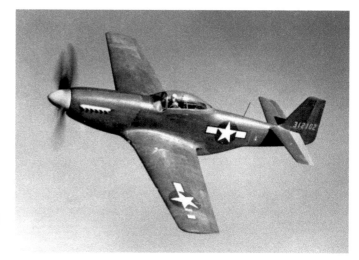

One of two P-51D
prototypes was a modified
P-51B-10-NA 42-12102 as
NA-106s in 1943. (NAA)

The North American P-51D Mustang's advanced cockpit compared with that of the A-36A Apache. (USAF)

Early production USAAF P-51D-5-NA 44-13366 without a dorsal fin, on a pre-delivery flight. (NAA)

CHAPTER TWO

In RAF Service

When the British Purchasing Commission ordered a new fighter aircraft off the drawing board of one of the youngest American plane makers in 1940, it had no idea it would become the most potent and versatile fighter aircraft of the Second World War.

The first of 320 Allison-powered North American Mustang Is entered Royal Air Force (RAF) service in April 1942 with No. 2 Squadron at Sawbridgeworth in the armed tactical reconnaissance role with Army Co-operation Command. Equipped with an F24 camera mounted obliquely aft of the pilot's seat on the port side, its first operational sortie took place on 27 July, subsequently photographing Dieppe before the failed raid took place in August.

Having replaced its Tomahawk IIAs with the Mustang I at West Zoyland in April 1942, No. 268 Squadron continued to operate the type for the next three years. In October the squadron's Mustang Is gained the distinction of becoming the first single-engined fighter based in England to penetrate beyond the German border during a raid on the Dortmund–Elms Canal and on 26 November during an operation over Holland. F/O R. A. Bethell, shot down a Luftwaffe Klemm trainer and a Junkers W-34 target tug, the squadron's first recorded air-to-air combat victories. In May and June 1943 the squadron operated from Odiham in southern England, conducting morning and evening patrols at low level to prevent low-flying enemy 'hit and run raiders' and reconnaissance aircraft from crossing over the English coast. In July 1943 the Squadron re-equipped with the Mustang IA, which played an active roles in Operation *Starkey* in preparations consistent with an assault on Boulogne that never happened during the period 27 August to 9 September 1943. In November the squadron moved to Turnhouse in Scotland, exchanging its Mustang IAs with those of No. 63 Squadron to conduct a period of training in preparation for the forthcoming invasion of occupied Europe in 1944.

Some 520 Mustangs, 92 Mustang IAs armed with four 20 mm cannon, and 50 Mustang IIs entered service with 20 RAF squadrons. 274 Merlin-engined

P-51Bs and 636 P-51Cs were supplied under the Lend-Lease agreement to the RAF as Mustang IIIs. They were delivered with their original close-framed cockpit canopies, many of which were replaced by the bulged, sliding frameless hood designed by R. Malcolm.

Four F-6A Mustangs were borrowed from the USAAF and used by No. 225 Squadron RAF for reconnaissance flights in Tunisia in April 1943 during Operation *Flax* to cut the air supply lines between Italy and the Axis armies in Tunisia.

During spring and summer 1943, No. 613 Squadron Mustang Is were flown on low-level shipping reconnaissance flights, codenamed 'Lagoons', over the North Sea, calling in heavy Coastal Command strike aircraft when enemy shipping was located. No. 168 Squadron did not become operational until it moved to Odiham in August 1943 and re-equipped the Mustang IA. It soon began operations with photo reconnaissance sorties along the French coast and 'Rhubarbs', in which aircraft flew at low level into France or Belgium to attack targets of opportunity on the ground.

The Mustang III initially equipped No. 65 Squadron in late December of 1943 at Gravesend, followed by No. 19 Squadron in March of 1944. Nos 65 and 122 Squadrons with Mustang IIIs were part of 122 Wing at Funtington on D-Day while No. 129 Squadron had became part of the 2nd Tactical Air Force in June 1943 and converted to the Mustang III in April 1944 in time for Operation *Overlord*. No. 112 Squadron was also heavily involved in D-Day operations and within a few weeks had moved to France to support the invasion, as did No. 168 Squadron, which flew over 500 sorties in July and August 1944 in support of the Allied ground forces. After re-equipping with the Mustang II in June 1944, No. 2 Squadron flew tactical reconnaissance sorties over the D-Day beaches before deploying to B10/Plumetot airfield in France in July. When W/C Leonard Cheshire commanded Bomber Command's elite No. 617 Squadron, targets were generally marked by Mosquito VIs, which he led. RAF records state that two RAF Mustang IIIs were allocated to Woodhall Spa on 22 June 1944, with Cheshire flying his first Mustang-marking mission on Siracourt on 25 June. Cheshire took off in Mustang III HB837 on 6 July to mark the V-3 long-range gun site at Mimoyecques in northern France for No. 617 Squadron's Lancasters to successfully bomb. It was his 100th mission and the next day he was told that his command of No. 617 was at an end and he was off operational flying. In September Leonard Cheshire was awarded the Victoria Cross.

On 5 May 1944, a major Allied bombing operation was carried out by No. 239 Wing in order to breach the hydro-electric dam on the Pescara River. It included Mustang IIIs of No. 260 Squadron based at Cutella in Italy, which dropped 500-lb bombs on the target.

No. 268 Squadron moved south in early 1944 as part of 35 (Reconnaissance) Wing of the 2nd Tactical Air Force based at North Weald. The squadron was responsible for obtaining some of the first low-level photography of V-1 launch sites in France. On D-Day, 6 June 1944, the squadron initially operated providing naval gunnery spotting and direction for units of the Home Fleet bombarding enemy defences operating from RNAS Lee-on-Solent. The squadron suffered only one recorded loss on D-Day.

After forming part of the 133 Polish Fighter Wing for D-Day, No. 129 Squadron's Mustang IIIs returned to RAF Brenzett, where it undertook 'Diver' operations against V-1 flying bombs. The squadron's top-scoring pilot was F/Lt Ruchwaldy with a score of ten V-1s destroyed. By 5 September 1944, RAF Mustangs had destroyed 232 V-1s, their high speed being invaluable for the 'Diver' operations.

In September, No. 234 Squadron converted to Mustang IIIs, which it used to provide long-range bomber escort missions from North Weald and after December 1944 from Bentwaters. On 1 May 1945 the squadron was moved to Peterhead to provide a similar service to the RAF Coastal Command strike wings operating along the Norwegian coast, having received some of the RAF's first Mustang IVs. No. 26 Squadron reverted to flying Mustang Is in December 1944 for reconnaissance missions over the Netherlands from Exeter and in April 1945 the Squadron spent two weeks spotting for French warships bombarding pockets of German resistance from Cognac before it converted to Spitfire XIVs in June 1945. In November 1944 No. 64 Squadron received the Mustang III and flew them for the rest of the war covering daylight raids of the RAF Bomber Command on Germany. After the end of hostilities the squadron moved to Horsham St Faith, receiving Mustang IVs in August 1945.

281 P-51Ds were supplied to the RAF as Mustang IVs, plus 594 Dallas-built P-51Ks fitted with the Aeroproducts airscrew. After D-Day operating from Funtington, No. 19 Squadron had started long-range escort duties from Peterhead in Scotland, for Coastal Command off the coast of Norway, before converting to the Mustang IV in April 1945.

Four Polish squadrons, Nos 306, 309, 315 and 316, had converted to Mustang IIIs in early 1944. As part of 133 Polish Fighter Wing, on 28 April No. 306 Squadron based at Coolham made the first of twenty-five operational Mustang 'Ramrod' sorties, attacking ground targets at will, while 'Ranger' operations flown over enemy territory in the hope of enticing the Luftwaffe into action, and 'Rodeo' fighter sweeps over enemy territory quickly became popular among pilots. On 9 July 1944, the Poles moved to Brenzett, where the invasion stripes were removed to help the aircraft in high-speed chases against V-1s, during which the squadron destroyed more than fifty flying bombs in five weeks.

On 12 December 1944, No. 309 Squadron joined 133 Polish Fighter Wing stationed at Andrews Field, and until the end of war the unit flew almost solely escort missions to various targets in Germany. On 9 April 1945, during an escort mission to Hamburg, the unit's pilots scored the last kills for the RAF during the war when F/Lt Gorzula, F/Lt Mencel and W/O Murkowski were each credited with one Me 262 destroyed, while F/O Lewandowski and P/O Mozolowski damaged another.

No. 315 (Polish) Squadron re-equipped with the Mustang III in March 1944. Based at Coolham, it formed part of southern England's defence against the V-1 flying bombs and operated over France during the Battle of Normandy, shooting down eight enemy aircraft and destroying several trains before moving to airfields in Normandy. On 18 August, twelve of the squadron's Mustangs engaged sixty German fighters of JG2 and JG26, which were in the process of taking off and landing at Beauvais, France. In the ensuing battle, the squadron claimed sixteen victories, one probable and three damaged with the loss of one pilot. The squadron later carried out operations over Germany, Norway and the Netherlands until the end of the war.

No. 316 (Polish) Squadron re-equipped with Mustang IIIs at Coltishall in April 1944 to carry out 'Ramrods' before moving to West Malling as part of Air Defence of Great Britain (ADGB) for 'Diver' patrol duties. In a six-week period the squadron shot down fifty-eight V-1s before moving back to Coltishall as part of 12 Fighter Group. The squadron took part in 'Rhubarb' raids over the Netherlands, 'Rangers' over Norway and Denmark and 'Rodeos' over Germany in 1945. During a 'Rodeo' sorties, one of its Mustangs landed in enemy territory, picked up a shot down comrade and flew back to base with one pilot sitting on the other. While escorting bombers over to Leipzig on 10 April, the squadron recorded its last success when F/O Walawski shot down two Me 210s, F/O Popiel scored one Me 210 destroyed and one probable, and then in another skirmish, together with Sgt Sypyrek F/O Popiel, damaged three Me 410s, while Sgt Tomaszewski damaged another. No. 303 (Polish) Squadron re-equipped with Mustang IVs in on 1 April 1945 and on 25 April the squadron escorted No. 617 Squadron's raid on Hitler's retreat at Berchtesgaden along with Nos 118, 442 and 611 Squadrons' Mustangs.

After three months of intense operations in France after D-Day, No. 112 Squadron's Mustang IIIs were withdrawn to England and continued providing long-range escorts to both Bomber Command and the United States 8th Air Force. In February 1945 it was based at Cervia in Italy with Mustang IVs and deployed to Prkos airfield in Zadar after attacking targets in Yugoslavia. On 17 May 1944, No. 213 Squadron had arrived at Idku in Egypt and set about converting to the Mustang, which it would operate until the end of the war. During its time with the Balkan Air Force the squadron flew both the Mustang III and IV as part of No. 281 Wing and was based at Prkos airfield in March 1945 to support the Yugoslav Fourth Army.

No 450 (RCAF) Squadron equipped with Mustang IIIs was based at Fano in Italy from November 1944 and conducted tactical reconnaissance and ground attack missions, its final operation being as part of Operation *Bowler*, an air attack on Venice harbour on 21 March 1945.

There were no fewer than fifteen Mustang squadrons in RAF Fighter Command at the end of the war, but the last of Mustang IVs of No. 64 Squadron at Horsham St Faith were withdrawn from service in February 1946, while overseas Mustang IVs remained with No. 213 Squadron at Nicosia in Cyprus until January 1947.

The British Air Commission had requested two lightweight development Mustangs, one XP-51F and an XP-51G, which were shipped to England in June 1944 and February 1945 respectively. Neither type went into production. They were followed by one P-51H, the last production version of the Mustang, which was sent for evaluation at Boscombe Down in 1945, serial KN98, but was not adopted by the RAF.

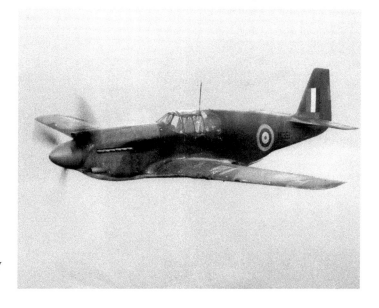

Above: The first Mustang I to be delivered to the RAF, AG346, served with Nos 225, 63 and 26 Squadrons. In 1944, it flew with Nos 16 and 168 Squadrons before it was shot down by flak over France on 20 August 1944. (NAA)

Right: Mustang I AG351 was used as a trials aircraft with the Air Fighting Development Unit (AFDU) at Boscombe Down in early 1942. (RAF)

Mustang I AM108 was another trials aircraft with the AFDU, seen with testing papier mache drop fuel tanks. (RAF)

No. 26 (Army Co-operative) Squadron was equipped with the Mustang I in January 1942 based at Gatwick. (RAF)

Two Mustang Is of No. II (AC) Squadron, which were received in April 1942. (RAF)

Right: A newly delivered Mustang I AG493 was delivered to No. 613 (City of Manchester) Squadron at Twinwood Farm in April 1942. (RAF)

Below: A No. II (AC) Squadron Mustang I AG 633 based at Sawbridgeworth in 1943. (F. Prins Collection)

EW998, the only A-36A to be delivered to the RAF and which was used for evaluation, seen carrying 500-lb GP bombs. (F. Prins Collection)

Mustang I AL958 on a pre-delivery test flight flown over California by Bob Chilton in October 1942. (NAA)

Some of the ninety-two Mustang IAs delivered to the RAF being prepared for shipment from Inglewood to Britain. (NA)

RAF and USAAF ground crew work on Mustang I AG411 at the USAAF Base Air Depot 1 at RAF Burtonwood. (USAF)

No. 268 Squadron Mustang IA FD474 armed with four 20-mm cannon at Mount Farm was transferred to the USAAF as an F6 in 1943. (IWM)

Left: No. 19 Squadron Mustang IIIs fitted with Malcolm hoods based at Ford in April 1944. (RAF)

Below: No. 315 (Polish) Squadron Mustang III FB123, flown by W/O Ryszard Idrian, escorts a No. 489 Squadron Beaufighter X on a shipping strike mission in July 1944. (RAF)

No. 26 Squadron
Mustang I with
nose art at Chateau
Bernad/Cognac in
France in April 1945.
(John Trathome)

Mustang IIIs of No. 316
(Polish) Squadron at
Coltishall in February
1945. (RAF)

A pair of
No. 260 Squadron
Mustang IIIs based
at Fano in Italy in
February 1945. (F. Prins
Collection)

Above: A No. 112 Squadron Mustang IV follows one of the squadron's Mustang IIIs at Cervia in March 1945. (IWM)

Left: RAF Mustang IV KH858 undergoing maintenance at RAF Fayid in Egypt in 1947. (A. L. Homersham)

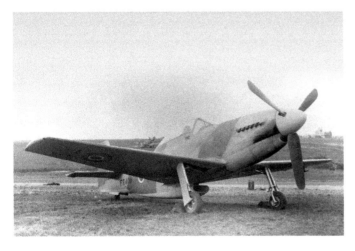

One of three lightweight XP-51F Mustangs built. FR409 was delivered to the RAF on 20 June 1944 and tested at the A&AEE at Boscombe Down. (RAF)

CHAPTER THREE

USAAF Service

When America entered the Second World War after the Japanese attack on Pearl Harbor, it began to show interest in the North American fighter by ordering 150 NA-97s, a version of the Mustang evolved specifically for dive-bombing. Designated A-36A and named Apache, it was fitted with wing-mounted airbrakes and underwing racks for two 500-lb bombs. It was armed with six 0.5-inch machine guns. The A-36As were followed by 310 P-51As, now named Mustangs, from March 1943, fifty of which were converted to F-6A and 'Bs fitted with K-24 cameras.

The A-36A first went into action with USAAF in July 1943 with the 27th and 86th Fighter Bomb Groups (FBG), based in North Africa, against targets in Sicily leading up to and following the Allied landings on the island. On 4 August, seventy-two A-36As operating in relays attacked enemy forces in the town of Troina for 13 hours, and in September A-36As sunk a 50,000-ton Italian transport vessel at Baguara.

The type was deployed to Benal in India in November with the 311st FBG, which undertook the first long-range escorts for American bombers attacking targets in the Rangoon area of Burma. A number of P-51As were issued to China-based USAAF fighter units, while others were deployed to the 107th Tactical Reconnaissance Squadron in England. However, the USAAF lost a total of seventy-three A-36As in 1943 mainly due to training accidents.

By this time, production of the Merlin-powered P-51B had begun and the first were delivered to the US 8th Air Force in England during late 1943. On 1 December the 354th Fighter Group (FG) flew its first operation over the French and Belgian coasts from Boxted. The group flew its first escort mission on 5 December with B-17s to the Amiens area and on 13 December it flew a round trip of 1,000 miles escorting B-17s to Kiel. Between 18 March and 1 April 1944 P-51Bs of the 4th FG claimed no less than 100 confirmed enemy aircraft destroyed plus eight probables while escorting USAAF B-17 on raids on Berlin. The group was formed from the RAF Eagle Squadrons established in 1940 and manned by American pilots.

The 339th FG provided fighter cover over the Channel and the coast of Normandy during the invasion of France in June 1944, strafing and dive-bombing enemy positions while Allied forces fought to break out of the beachhead in France. On 4 July, the Commander-in-Chief of the Allied invasion forces, General Dwight D. Eisenhower, flew a personal reconnaissance of the Saint-Lo area in a 356th FS twin-seat P-51B from A2 airfield near Cricqueville-en-Bessin.

The bubble canopied P-51D had begun to arrive in Europe in quantity in March 1944 and the 55th FG was the first to get the new Mustang to replace its P-38s. The 31st and 52nd FGs of the 15th Air Force were the first units to re-equip with P-51Ds in Italy and on 21 April the 31st FG escorted B-24s raiding the oil refineries at Pliesti in Romania. Near Bucharest, sixty German fighters attacked the B-24s and in the ensuing battle its pilots claimed seventeen enemy fighters destroyed, seven probables and ten damaged for the loss of only one of their own.

By mid-1944, more than 5,000 Mustangs equipped the 8th Air Force in the European Theater of Operations (ETO). Its 1st, 2nd and 3rd Air Divisions each had a fighter wing that comprised six fighter groups within which were three fighter squadrons.

When Capt Bert Marshall belly landed his 355th FG P-51D in a field near Soissons in France after being hit by flak on 18 August 1944, his colleague 2nd Lt Royce Priest landed nearby to pick him up. Sitting on Marshall's lap, Priest took off and flew home to their base at Steeple Morden in England. Marshall finished the war with seven air-to-air victories and Priest with five.

During the Battle of the Bulge, a detachment of the 352nd FG moved to Asch Airfield in Belgium placed under the control of the 9th Air Force. On 25 December 1944, the commanding officer of the group's 328th FS, Major George E. Preddy Jr, was shot down and killed by 'friendly fire' after shooting down two Bf 109s. With twenty-six-and-a-half air-to-air victories, he would be the top scoring P-51 Mustang pilot of the Second World War.

On 1 January 1945 Germany launched Operation *Bodenplatte* to gain air superiority during a stagnant stage of the Battle of the Bulge. The 352nd FG's deputy commander, Col John C. Meyer, anticipated the attack and had a flight of twelve 487th FS Mustangs ready to take off when the attack began. As they readied for takeoff, the airfield was attacked by Bf 109s and Fw 190s fighters from JG 11 and the Mustangs took off under fire. In the ensuing battle, the 352nd FG shot down almost half the enemy aircraft without loss. Col Meyer shot down two Fw 190s adding to his score of twenty-four aerial victories.

The 357th FG based at Leiston claimed fifty-six air victories on 14 January 1944, the highest single-day claim by a British-based USAAF group. The group's final victory would be an Me 262, shot down on 19 April 1945 by 2nd Lt James P. McMullen of the 364th FS.

On 8 March, Major Pierce W. McKennon, commanding officer of the 4th FG's 335th FS based at Debden, was rescued from a field deep in Germany by his wingman Lt George D. Green after being shot down while attacking ground targets near Berlin. He finished the war credited with twelve aerial victories.

The 78th FG based at Duxford converted to P-51Ds in December 1944 and participated in the Battle of the Bulge until January 1945 and supported the airborne assault across the Rhine in March. The group received a Distinguished Unit Citation for destroying numerous German aircraft on five airfields near Prague and Pilsen on 16 April 1945. On 25 April RAF Lancasters bombed Hitler's mountain chalet and SS barracks at Berchtesgaden escorted by the group's P-51Ds.

The 31st FG's 307th, 308th and 309th FSs based at San Servo in Italy converted to P-51Ds in April 1944. They escorted the 15th Air Force B-24 bomber raids on Ploesti and on 22 July escorted P-38 Lightning strafing the oil Romanian oil fields and landed at Piryatin in Russia. After leaving Piryatin three days later they encountered a large formation of Ju 87 Stukas heading for the Russian lines and destroyed twenty-seven of them.

The wing took part in the invasion of southern France in August 1944 and between December 1944 and March 1945, pilots of the 31st FG's 308th FS shot down seven Me 262s during bomber escort missions over Germany. The group achieved the highest score in the 15th Air Force with 571 enemy aircraft destroyed.

Between 1941 and 1945, African American pilots had been trained at a segregated air base in Tuskegee, Alabama. The most famous of the Tuskegee airmen were those of the 332nd FG, known as the 'Red Tails' for the distinctive markings of their aircraft. Initially flying as part of the 15th Air Force in North Africa, the group moved to Ramitelli airfield on the Adriatic coast of Italy to fly long-range bomber escort missions into central and eastern Europe. The 332nd FG was awarded the Presidential Unit Citation for its longest bomber escort mission to Berlin, a 1,600-mile round trip, on 24 March 1945 during which its pilots destroyed three Me 262s and damaged another five for the loss of two Mustangs. The group's 99th, 100th, 101st and 302nd FSs flew more than 15,000 sorties, shooting down 112 enemy aircraft for the loss of sixty pilots.

F-6B Mustangs served with the 9th Air Force's 107th Tactical Reconnaissance Squadron (TRS) while 10th Tactical Reconnaissance Group's 12th and 15th TRSs equipped with F-6Bs and 'Cs were based at Chalgrove in June 1944. In August the F-6s operated from airstrips at St Dizier and Conflans in France. In April 1945 another F-6 TRS was added, the 162nd. On 8 May, the day that hostilities in Europe officially ended, two 162nd F-6s patrolling the Danube were attacked by Fw 190s. They shot down one, which was the last Luftwaffe aircraft to fall in combat over Europe. The 162nd TFS also flew the last USAAF operational sortie in the ETO.

The 355th FG's P-51s destroyed more enemy aircraft on the ground than any other 8th Air Force group, while the 359th FG claimed 253 enemy aircraft in the air and 98 on the ground. In the ETO alone, the P-51s were credited with 4,950 air combat victories claimed by USAAF pilots and with 4,131 enemy aircraft claimed as destroyed on the ground.

In February 1944, the recently formed US 1st Air Commandos equipped with P-51As embarked on a secret mission launched from a remote airstrip in India to attack Japanese ground targets behind enemy lines in Burma. The 1st Air Commandos were then tasked to support the Chindits, special operations units of the British and Indian armies, in a mission known as Operation *Thursday*, which continued until August. During the campaign the 1st Air Commando Mustangs flew 1,482 combat missions and lost five aircraft.

During the siege of Myitkyina in northern Burma in May 1944, A-36As and P-51s of the 311th FBG supported a US and Chinese advance until the town was recaptured on 3 August. During the British offensive in the summer of 1944, which was supported by USAAF, Mustangs destroyed thirty-one Japanese aircraft on the ground at Don Muang near Bangkok after a flight of 780 miles to the target. Following a major Japanese offensive in China, the US 14th Air Force increased its strength with Composite Wings in November equipped with P-47s and P-51s.

In November, the USAAF's 82nd TRS at Morotai, a small island in the Netherlands East Indies, began to replace its P-40s with the F-6D. This was the first Mustang variant to see service in the Pacific Operational Area and it was followed by the 110th TRS in February 1945.

During a reconnaissance mission from Leyte to Luzon in the Philippines on 11 January 1945, two F-6Ds of the 71st TRG's 82nd TRS intercepted twelve Japanese Zeros escorting a Betty bomber. Capt. William A. Shomo destroyed six fighters and 2nd Lt Paul Lipscombe claimed another three. The two pilots were awarded the Congressional Medal of Honour and Distinguished Flying Cross respectively.

P-51Ds of VII Fighter Command's 15th and 21st FGs began operations from Iwo Jima in May 1945, maintaining constant air patrols from dawn and dusk while P-51Ds of the 548th Night Fighter Squadron flew during the night. 108 P-51Ds based at Iwo Jima escorted B-29s in an attack on the Nakajima-Musashi factory near Tokyo on 7 April, the first time that US land-based fighters had flown over the Japanese home islands. During the mission, they shot down twenty-one Japanese fighter aircraft for the loss only two Mustangs. Each P-51D carried two 165 US-gallon drop tanks on this and subsequent 1,500-mile escort missions. Mustangs strafed enemy airfields in Okinawa using high-velocity aircraft rockets (HVAR) on 17 April and while escorting a daylight B-29 raid on Yokohama on 29 May, 150 enemy fighters were engaged by 101 P-51Ds, which shot down twenty-six Japanese aircraft for the loss of three of their number. On 1 June, 149 P-51Ds were despatched on an escort mission to Kobe. However, severe thunderstorms were encountered en route and twenty-seven were lost, mostly in mid-air collisions. Five days after the second atomic bomb was dropped on Nagasaki on 9 August, B-29s escorted by 186 P-51Ds attacked a naval base at Hikari, an army arsenal at Osaka and an oil plant a Atika. The next day, Japan surrendered unconditionally.

An early production cannon-armed P-51A, 41-37427 was converted to an F-6A with two K-24 cameras in USAAF service. (NA)

An A-36A Apache used for pilot training at Harding Field at Baton Rouge, Louisiana, in 1942. (USAF)

Three A-36A Apaches from Harding Field on a training mission over Louisiana in November 1943. (USAF)

Personnel of the 527th FBS, 86th FBG, with A-36A Apache 42-84067 in Sicily loaded up with a 500-lb bomb. It was lost in January 1944. (USAF)

P-51A-10-NA 43-6246 belonging to the Army Air Forces Tactical Center in Orlando, Florida, in 1943. (USAF)

P-51B-1-NA 41-312201 was assigned to 54th FG at Bartow Army Airfield in Florida for pilot training. (NA)

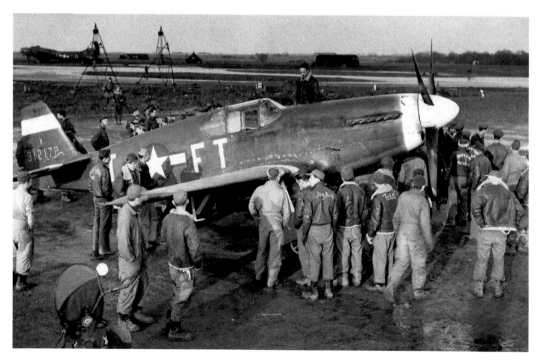

USAAF B-17 airmen inspecting a P-51B of the 353rd FS, 345th FG, the first USAAF Mustang unit to he deployed to England in December 1943. (USAF)

P-51B-1-NA *Miss Pea Ridge* 43-12433 from the 356th FFS, 354th FG 'Pioneer Mustang Group', originally delivered to the RAF as Mustang III FX905. (USAF)

Capt. Howard L. Lambert was lost over the North Sea on 29 March 1944 flying the 355th FS, 357th FS, P-51B 43-6508. (NRO)

Don Gentile's P-51B *Shangri-La*. Assigned to 336FS, 4FG, 8AF USAAF. He claimed seven-and-a-half of his twenty-one victories in this aircraft before he crashed it during a display at his home base, Debden, on 13 April 1944. (USAF)

376th FS, 361st FG, P-51Bs taking off from RAF Bottisham on D-Day 6 June 1944. (USAF)

A 354th FS, 355th FG, P-51B *The Iowa Beaut*, fitted with a Malcolm Hood, was flown by Lt Robert J. Hulderman from Steeple Morden in July 1944. (USAF)

Above: The 328th FS, 352nd FG, P-51B 42-106703 *Snoot's Sniper* at Mount Farm flown by Lt Francis W. Horne. (USAF)

Left: A 375th FS, 361st FG, P-51D 44-13926 shows off its Invasion Stripes in July 1944. (USAF)

Lt Darwin Berry's P-51D of the 4th FS, 52nd FG, at Debden in July 1944. (USAF)

Four 362nd FS, 357th FG, P-51D-5-Nas based at Leiston, including Lt Harvey Mace's *Sweet Helen II* and 44-13334 *Wee Willy II* flown by Capt. Calvert Williams. (USAF)

P-51D-5-NA 44-13518 *Horse's Itch* of Maj. Edwin W. Hiro, CO of the 363rd FS, 357th FG, based in Leiston, killed in action in September 1944. (USAF)

Yellow-nosed P-51Ds and P-51Bs of the 374th FS, 361st FG, based at Little Walden. (USAF)

375th FS, 361st FG, P-51D *Lou IV* P-51D-5-NA of Lt Col Thomas J. J. Christian Jr, who was killed while attacking Arras marshaling yards on 12 August 1944. (USAF)

Lt Stanley F. Fierstein landing his 111st TRS, 68th FG, F-6C *Val Gal* at Lyon-Bron in France in September 1944. (USAF)

P-51Ds at the Bottisham Group Commander conference in October 1944, 79th FS, 20th FG, 44-14337 *Gentle Annie* and 44-14111 *Straw Boss 2*. (NA)

P-51C VF-T assigned to the 336th FS, 4th FG fitted with a Malcolm canopy and paper drop tanks at Debden in September 1944. (USAF)

Capt. Shelton Monroe's P-51D *T-Wang* in the 335th FS, 4th FG, Narvik dispersal area at Debden in March 1945. (USAF)

Lt Leroy Pletz landing at Raydon in his 352nd FS, 353rd FG, P-51K 44-11624 *Donna Mite*, code SX-M. (NA)

P-51D (CV-Q) of the 359th FG, (LC-D) of the 20th FG, (LH-V) of the 353rd FG and (C5-Q) of the 357th FG, at Debden, home of the 4th FG in March 1945. (Edward Richie)

Capt. Frank E. Birtciel's 343rd FS, 55th FG, P-51D *Miss Velma* based at Kings Ciffe in April 1945. (USAF)

Lt Carrol Ofshun's
363rd FS, 357th FG, P-51
44-14977 *The Count* lines
up for take-off from
Leiston. (USAF)

F-6K Mustangs of the
22th TRS, 69th TRG, based
at Nancy-Orchy in France
in March 1945. (NA)

Lt Col Glenn Eagleston
briefing 354th FG pilots
before they take off from
Ober Olm, Germany, on
a mission over enemy
territory in April 1945.
(USAF)

Servicing a 355th FS, 354th FG, P-51D at the bomb-damaged Ober Olm airfield in Germany in April 1945. (USAF)

A post-VJ Day line-up of 83rd FS, 78th FG, P-51K Mustangs at Duxford in June 1945. (USAF)

A P-51C of the 5th FS, 52nd FG, Fifteen Air Force, at Torretto airfield, Italy, in March 1945. (USAF)

Right: P-51D 44-13287 *Miss Ruth* of the 5th FS, 52nd FG, with 44-13263 *Jo-Baby* in the background over Italy. (USAF)

Below: P-51D 44-13217 *Tempus Fugit* of the 308th FS, 31st FG, Fifteenth Air Force, at San Severo in Italy. (USAF)

P-51D Mustangs of the
Fifteenth Air Force's 31st
FG (WZ-8), 325th FG (00)
and 332nd FG (7), flying
over Italy in 1945. (USAF)

A USAAF armourer loading
a 12.7 mm ammunition
belt in the wing of a 100th
FS, 332 FG, 15th Air Force,
P-51 at Foggia, Italy,
with P-51C *Stinky* in the
background. (NA)

Lt Charles White 301st FS, 332nd FG, P-51D
Creamer's Dream at Ramitelli, Italy, in January
1945. (LOC)

Above: P-51D
44-15648 *Lollipoop II*
of the 100th FS, 332nd
FG, at Cattulca, Italy.
(USAF)

Right: 1st Air
Commando Group
P–51A Mustangs at
Hailakandi, India, in
1944. (USAF)

Maj. Robert Smith's
1st Air Commando
Group's P-51A
43-6151 *Barbie* being
serviced at Hailakandi,
India. (USAF)

A 311th FBG Tenth Air Force P-51A 43-6109 at Tingkawk Sakan, Burma, in 1944. (USAF)

A 26th FS, 51st FG, Fourteenth Air Force, F-6C Mustang at Kunming, China, in 1945. (USAF)

Lt Lester Arasmith's 530th FS, 311th FG, Fourteenth Air Force, P-51C 42-103896 *Princess* over China in 1945. (NA)

P-51D *My Ned* of the 530th
FS, 311th FG, based at
Hsian, China, in June 1945.
(NA)

P-51Bs and P-51Cs of the
118th TRS, 23rd FG, at
Laohwangping Airfield,
Guizhou Province, in June
1945. (San Diego Air and
Space Museum)

Seventy-nine P-51Ds ferried from the United
States to Guam on board the carrier USS
Kalinin Bay in March 1945. (US Navy)

P-51Ds of the 39th FS, 35th FG, and P-47Ds undergo maintenance at Lingayen airfield in the Philippines in April 1945. (USAF)

A P-51D of the 47th FS, 15th FG, on a barge bound for Iwo Jima in April 1945. (USAF)

P-51D 44-63909 and 44-72672 of the 458th FS, 506th FG, on Iwo Jima in June 1945. (USAF)

A 562nd FS, 506th FG, P-51D pushed in the dispersal area on Iwo Jima fitted with a double antenna, which is the Uncle Dog system that helped the Mustangs navigate over very long-range missions. (NA)

P-51Ds of the 531st FS, 21st FG, assembled at South Field, Iwo Jima. P-51D 44-63915 *330* was shot down near Nariamasu Airfield, Japan, on 28 July 1945. (USAF)

CHAPTER FOUR

Post-war European and Middle East Operators

France

On 1 January 1945, the French Air Force Groupe de Reconnaissance (GR) II/33 'Savoie' became an Allied tactical photographic unit based at Nancy and the Americans agreed to supply it with twenty P-51s. All were conversions from P-51Cs or P-51Ds to F-6Cs or F-6Ds equipped with K-17, K-22 and K-24 cameras. Between 16 April and 8 May 1945, VE Day, the 'Savoie' group flew 189 sorties, most of which were long-range reconnaissance missions on the retreating Wermacht's communication lines. On 9 May 1945, nine GR II/33 Mustangs took part in the VE Day flypast over the Champs-Elysées.

With the return to peace, the group's pilots left Nancy for Fribourg on 12 September 1945, and were replaced by pilots of the GR I/33 'Belfort' Group. Some of the Mustangs were deployed to Blida in Algeria between February and April 1946 tasked with mapping northern Africa. In April 1950, the 'Savoie' group moved to Cognac.

Mustangs were also allocated to GR I/33 'Belfort' and by February 1949 the unit had four F-5Fs, ten F-5Gs and six F-6Cs. One F-6C was stationed permanently in Lahr with Escadrille de Liaison Aérienne (ELA) 55, operating as liaison aircraft. All GR I/33 Mustangs were grounded in July 1950. GR II/33 kept flying its Mustangs extensively and in November 1951 it left for Weisbaden to take part in the FTX51 combined maneuvers. However, a year later the first F-84F Thunderjets were being delivered and from January 1953, its remaining eight Mustangs were withdrawn from service by September. They were flown to Rennes and returned to the Americans; they were subsequently scrapped. A few Mustangs were sent to Ambérieu for ground instruction, marking the end of the type's career in the French Air Force.

Italy

The Peace Treaty of Paris of 1947 placed severe restrictions on all of the Italian armed forces, but the establishment of NATO in 1949 with Italy as a founding member brought about the necessity for the modernisation of the Italian Air Force (AMI). As part of America's Mutual Defense Assistance Program, between September 1947 and January 1951, 173 P-51D were delivered to the AMI. The first Mustangs arrived at the Gruppo Scuola Volo at Lecce Air Base in the spring of 1949 and the P-51Ds were subsequently operated by five reactivated AMI fighter wings: 2, 3, 4, 6, and 51 Stormos.

From 1948 to 1953, only forty-eight P-51Ds remained in service and phasing out of the Mustang began in summer 1958. AMI P-51Ds had participated in a UN mission in Somalia and in 1950 six of them were donated to the embryonic Somalian Air Force. However, all the surviving Mustangs were returned to Italy before Somalia gained its independence in June 1960.

Switzerland

After the Second World War the Swiss Air Force operated an ageing fleet of piston engine fighters including the Messerschmitt Bf 109E/G and Morane-Saulnier D-3801, and needed more capable aircraft to replace them. An order had been placed for de Havilland Vampire jet fighters, but they would not enter operational service until 1949. As a stopgap, a Swiss delegation signed a contract in December 1947 for 130 surplus USAAF P-51Ds at a reported price of US $4,000 each.

The P-51Ds were operated by five Swiss Air Force squadrons from 1948 to 1957, flying initially in the air defence role, and later in the ground attack role until airframe and engine fatigue meant they were no longer viable to continue to operate. The surviving Mustangs went into storage and were officially retired in April 1958. Many were scrapped in 1959/60 while a number were used for target practice on Swiss Army firing ranges into the 1970.

Sweden

When the Swedish Parliament in 1942 decided to set up five new fighter units, the domestic aviation industry could not cover the need for new aircraft. During the Second World War a number of USAAF P-51s landed in Sweden and in April 1945 two P-51Ds were taken over by the Royal Swedish Air Force (RSwAF), designated J 26.

After the end of the Second World War, the prices of surplus military aircraft fell sharply. In 1945 the Swedish Civil Aviation Administration bought fifty P-51Ds for US $8,240 each. A year later, it purchased another ninety by which time the price had dropped to US $ 1.675 per aircraft. In RSwAF service, they served with F 16 Wing at Uppsala and F 4 at Ostersund. In 1951 twelve were converted to reconnaissance aircraft, designated S 26 and served with F 21 Wing at Lulea. Nearly a quarter the J 26 fleet was lost in accidents in four years of operations.

From 1952, the RSwAF began to take the J 26 out of service. A total of forty-two were sold to the Dominican Air Force (FAD) and twenty-five to the Israel Defence Force/Air Force (IDF/AF), which took part in the Sinai campaign with great success. In November 1954, twenty-six J 26s were sold to the Nicaraguan Air Force (FAN) and served until 1965, after which a number were sold to the Maco Sales Corp in the USA.

Israel

The Israeli Air Force (IAF) was officially formed on 28 May 1948 with a variety of used combat aircraft procured both legally and illegally. Israeli agents in the USA had managed to purchase four P-51Ds, which were shipped to Israel despite the arms embargo. The first pair of Mustangs were rushed into service with the IAF's first fighter squadron stationed at Herzelia. Its superior range enabled the P-51Ds to conduct reconnaissance missions all over the Middle East without them being threatened by Arab fighter aircraft. The Mustang was also used in strike and interception missions and on 20 November 1948 a Mustang was scrambled from Castina to intercept and shoot down an RAF Mosquito PR.34, the first victim of an Israeli P-51. While escorting three T-6 Harvards on a strike mission on 7 January 1949, two Mustangs were intercepted by six MC.205s. In the ensuing dogfight, they shot down three Egyptian fighters.

After the end of the War of Independence in July 1949, four Mustangs began regular service in the new Israel Defence Force/Air Force (IDF/AF). In the early 1950s, thirty-six more P-51Ds were acquired in the USA, and in June 1952 twenty-five were purchased from Sweden. They were followed in 1955 by another batch of thirty from Italy.

With a total of seventy-nine operational P-51Ds and twenty-six airframes in Israel, the Mustangs were to see action again in 1951 against Syrian forces.

As the IDF/AF introduced jet fighters into service, many of the Mustangs were put into storage in 1956. Only the 116th Squadron's P-51Ds remained in service to train new pilots. However, with the outbreak of the Suez crisis in October 1956, forty-eight P-51Ds were reintroduced into operational service with a second squadron. If the performance of the Mustang was inferior to that of modern jets, IDF/AF Mustangs were tasked with the destruction of Egyptian fighters and bombers at remote bases, at ranges that could not be reached by its jet fighters.

On 29 October, the Mustangs were equipped with a weight attached to a cable, which was to be hung from the aircraft's tail to cut the enemy's telephone lines.

Four Mustangs were equipped as 'cable-cutters' and took off around noon, but upon arrival at the target, some had lost their equipment. Instead of aborting their mission, the pilots decided to cut the cable with their propellers and wings. This was particularly dangerous but the mission was a success.

The Mustangs flew 184 missions during the Suez crisis campaign, losing only seven aircraft, most to Egyptian ground fire. On 15 January 1961, the P-51D Mustang, the IDF/AF's last piston-engined combat aircraft, retired from service.

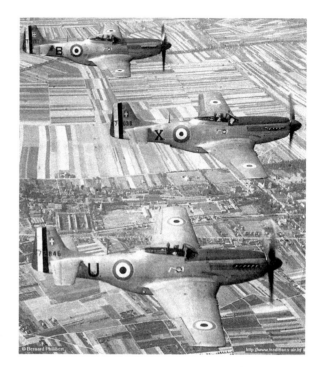

Right: Three French Air Force Groupe de Reconnaissance (GR) II/33 'Savoie' F-6D Mustangs in 1948. (French Air Force)

Below: Swiss Air Force F-6K Mustang leading a P-51D over Lake Thun in 1950. (Swiss Mustangs)

A P-51D Mustang of Gruppo Scuola Volo (training squadron) based at Lecce, the first of which arrived in the spring of 1949. (Caliaro Collection)

P-51D Mustangs were delivered to 4 Stormo as part of the US Mutual Defense Assistance Program (ItAF)

6 Stormo was reconstituted with P-51D Mustangs at Treviso on 1 January 1951. (F Ballista)

USAAF P-51D-5-NA CF-I 44-13345 *Mary Ann* force landed in Sweden in 1944 and later flew with the RSwAF F16 Wing, serial 26003. (via Leif Hellstrom)

USAAF 335th FS P51B-5-NA 43-6365 *Z Hub* landed at Rinkaby on 13 May 1944, which became the RSwAF's first Mustang, serial 26001. (RSwAF)

A surplus USAAF RSwAF P-51D Mustang, designated J 26 of F16 Wing at Uppsala. (RSwAF)

IDF/AF P-51D 3604, ex-USAAF 44-72208, RSwAF 26114, during delivery flight from Sweden to Israel in 1952. (Swiss Mustangs)

CHAPTER FIVE

Asia Pacific Operators

China

When the United States entered the Second World War, plans were made to provide the Republic of China Air Force (ROCAF) with modern American warplanes including P-51s. The Mustangs were initially flown by pilots of the Chinese-American Composite Wing (CACW), starting from November 1944 with P-51Bs and P-51Cs, but in February 1945 with P-51Ds and P-51Ks. After VJ Day, the government of Nationalist China bought almost the total American P-51 stocks in South-East Asia. Large numbers of the Mustangs were used during the civil war and the Nationalist forces eventually managed to evacuate 110 Mustangs to Taiwan in 1949, which provided the bulk of its newly created Republic of China Air Force (ROCAF) fighter strength throughout the subsequent years.

However, this was not before many of their pilots had defected, leaving a substantial number of Mustangs and Packard-built V-1650 Merlin engines behind. The People's Liberation Army (PLA) obtained its first Mustang in September 1948 when Capt. Yang Peiguang from the Nationalist 4th FG based in Beijing defected with his P-51D to the Communist forces in Jilin Province. With the Communist victory at the Battle of Jinzhou in October, thirty-one Mustangs were found in various states of repair at the Jinzhou airfield.

When Shenyang was captured by the PLA at the end of October, its Beiling airport was officially established as the People's Liberation Army Air Force (PLAAF) Repair Factory Number 5, and the first aircraft to be repaired were a total of thirty-six Mustangs. The last Mustang to fall into the PLA's hands occurred on 14 January 1949 when Lt Yan Chengyin from the Nationalist 3rd FG defected from his base at Nanjing to Communist-held Jinan.

The PLAAF formed its first squadron at the Beijing Nanyuan airfield on 15 August 1949 with six P-51s. The squadron was assigned the task of defending

Beijing's airspace from Nationalist forces and when Mao Zedong proclaimed the establishment of the People's Republic of China on 1 October 1949, the Soviet-style military parade in Beijing included a flypast by nine PLAAF Mustangs.

By 1950 the Soviet Union began supplying the Chinese with more modern equipment and by mid-August the PLAAF's surviving Mustangs were issued to Aviation School No.7, thirteen of which were modified to two-seat trainers. By September 1953, most Mustangs were retired from service, although eight remained in service to train Ilyushin Il-10 pilots on how to taxi their aircraft.

The Philippines

The Philippine Army Air Corps (PAAC) purchased over 150 refurbished F-51D Mustangs from US Government surplus stocks in the early 1950s to equip the 5th FW's 6th 'Cobras' and the 7th 'Bulldogs' and would continue with the renamed Philippine Air Force (PAF) as a frontline fighter until 1960. They saw combat against communist insurgents and rebels as counter insurgency (COIN) aircraft over the next two decades.

At one point, the PAF had more P-51 Mustang fighter aircraft than it had pilots and many were put into storage. However, the quality of the aircraft was matched by the superb flying skills of some of its more experienced pilots, as epitomised by four P-51D of the PAF's 'Blue Diamonds' flight demonstration team, which was formed in 1953.

Indonesia

From late 1945, Netherlands East Indies Army Air Force (ML-KNIL) squadrons equipped with P-51Ds fought against Indonesian nationalists during the Indonesian National Revolution. Nos 120, 121 and 122 Squadrons lost six Mustangs between 1947 and 1949 during operations *Product* and *Kraal*, but when the Dutch armed forces left the Netherland East Indies the Mustangs were handed over to the Indonesians in 1950.

Political instability meant that the new Indonesian Air Force (AURI) saw action against regional rebellions such as the Permesta, which, under the aegis of the Revolutionary Government of the Republic of Indonesia (PRRI), controlled northern Sulawesi. The CIA decided to support the Permesta and launch a clandestine operation codenamed 'Haik'. In March 1958 three F-51Ds were taken from the Philippine Air Force, together with some pilots recruited for the operation under the control of Civilian Air Transport (CAT), an American CIA front company.

Several AURI P-51D pilots scored their first kills during the operation, including Capt. Ignatius Dewanto, who shot down a rebel air force (AUREV) B-26 Invader over Ambon. Its CIA pilot, Allen Pope, was captured and tried in Jakarta and the operation was abandoned.

When Indonesia gained its independence in December 1949, the Dutch retained sovereignty over the western part of the island of New Guinea and took steps to prepare it for independence as a separate country. On December 1961, Indonesia's President Sukarno declared Operation *Trikora* aimed to seize and annex West New Guinea. To achieve air superiority, preparations were undertaken by the AURI to repair former Japanese wartime airstrips that had fallen into disrepair along the borders of Maluki and West New Guinea, which would be used for Indonesian infiltration operations.

During the operation, seven AURI P-51Ds were deployed to Laha airbase at Ambon. One was lost due to engine failure during the ferry flight from Makassar and the pilot died after bailing out into high seas. However, after negotiations, the Netherlands signed the New York Agreement with Indonesia on 15 August 1962, relinquishing control of West New Guinea to the United Nations.

AURI P-51Ds were used against British Commonwealth forces during the Indonesian confrontation, which began in 1963 and latest until August 1966. A total of sixty P-51D Mustangs were assigned to the AURI. The last to be deployed for military purposes were five Cavalier II Mustangs and one TF-51D delivered to Indonesia between 1972 and 1973. By 1985, only six AURI Mustangs remained in service.

Australia

The Royal Australian Air Force (RAAF) first operated the P-51 when No. 3 Squadron attached to the Desert Air Force replaced its P-40 Kittyhawks with RAF-supplied Mustang IIIs and IVs in November 1944, which saw extensive action during the Allied advance through Italy and Yugoslavia. The squadron was disbanded in July 1946. At the end of the war in the Pacific, the RAAF was reduced to one fighter wing with CA-17 and CA-18 Mustangs produced by the Commonwealth Aircraft Corporation (CAC). An initial order for 550 was reduced to 200. The air component of Allied Occupation Force in Japan included Mustangs from three squadrons, Nos 76, 77, and 82 of No 81 Wing at Iwakuni in April 1946.

In 1943, the Australian government arranged for the CAC to manufacture the P-51D under license from North American Aviation. Due to delays in the supply of components and engines, a total of 298 lend-lease P-51Ds and P-51Ks were procured, and in addition the RAAF also accepted Mustangs for the Netherlands East Indies Air Force.

The first eighty Mustang Mk 20s were assembled from 100 sets of semi-completed P-51D components supplied by North American Aviation with used Packard Merlin V-1650-3 engines, under the CA-17 designation.

A prototype Mustang, A68-1001, was used for development trials and the first CAC Mustang, A68-1, flew on 29 April 1945. This aircraft was delivered to the RAAF on 4 June 1945 and was used for trials by No. 1 Aircraft Performance Unit. It was placed in storage until 1953, when it was delivered to the Department of Supply at Woomera. A68-1 was one of six retired Mustangs selected to be made operational for a ferry flight to the remote Emu claypan in the South Australian desert where top secret preparations were under way for Project 'Totem', British atomic bomb tests. The Mustangs were placed some distance from the blast site to evaluate the effects. None sustained blast damage but were left when the Emu site was abandoned due to high radioactivity levels. The six Mustangs were salvaged during 1967 by an Adelaide syndicate and shipped to US where all but A68-1, which was built to fly again in 1980, were used only for parts by the Cavalier Aircraft Corp.

A second contract called for 170 improved Mustangs, but only 120 were completed. Known as CA-18, the first forty were built as Mustang Mk 21s with Packard Merlin V-1650-7 engines. The remaining CA-18s comprised fourteen Mk 22 reconnaissance versions. The Mk 23 used Rolls-Royce Merlin 66 or 70s while a contract for 250 Mk 24s was cancelled.

RAAF Mustangs had been assigned to Japan for occupation duties and in 1946, Nos 76, 77 and 82 Squadrons flew into Iwakuni. In 1949 Nos 76 and 82 Squadrons withdrew to Australia in 1949 while the Mustangs of No. 77 Squadron remained to take part in the Korean War from June 1950 until April 1951, when they were replaced by Gloster Meteors.

Mustangs remained in service with Citizen's Air Force Squadrons until they were withdrawn from service in 1959 and replaced by the CAC CA-27 Sabre.

New Zealand

The Royal New Zealand Air Force (RNZAF) received thirty P-51D Mustangs in 1945 from the United States as part of the planned replacement of its Corsair fighter aircraft. It was intended that it would receive a total of 370 Mustangs; however, these were cancelled when the war finished. The initial aircraft were placed in storage until 1951, when they were issued to the four squadrons of the Territorial Air Force (TAF), Otago, Canterbury, Wellington and Auckland.

No. 42 Squadron was reformed in 1946 at Ohakea equipped with P-51D Mustangs for fighter affiliation, communications, continuation flying and providing high-speed towing of banner targets, especially for RNZAF de Havilland Vampire jets. A few were issued to No. 14 Squadron at Ohakea in 1952 for target towing and specialist weapons courses. The majority were withdrawn from service in 1955 and again placed in storage, with most being sold for scrap in 1958 after the TAF was disbanded. The last RNZAF P-51D Mustang flight took part on 30 May 1957.

People's Liberation Army Air Force formed its first squadron at the Beijing Nanyuan airfield on 15 August 1949 with former Nationalist P-51Ds. (PLAAF)

Above: Many former USAF F-51Ds were delivered to the ROKAF after the Korean War. (USAF)

Right: Former USAF P-51D 45-11389 of the Philippine Air Force's 8th Fighter Squadron in 1957.

Netherlands East Indies Army Air Force (ML-KNIL) P-51Ds of 121 Squadron fought against Indonesian nationalists from 1945.

A 122 Squadron ML-KNIL P-51D that was handed over to the Indonesians in 1950.

Mustang IIIs of RAAF No. 3 Squadron based in Italy and attached to the Desert Air Force at the end of the Second World War. (RAAF)

RAAF No. 2 Squadron former USAAF P-51Ds flying off Lebuan in November 1945. (RAAF)

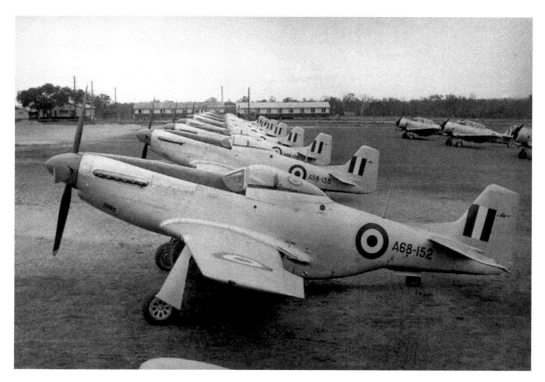

CA-18 Mk 23 Mustangs belonging to No. 2 OTU RAAF at Mildura that was reformed in 1952. (via Bruce Potts)

The first CA-17 Mk 20, A68-1, abandoned at the Emu atomic bomb test site, South Australia, in June 1967. (Geoff Goodall)

RNZAF P-51D Mustangs of No. 3 (Canterbury) TAF Squadron based at RNZAF Station Wigram. (Les Billcliff)

CHAPTER SIX

Korean War

The Korean War began on 25 June 1950 when North Korea invaded South Korea following clashes along the 38th Parallel and insurrections in South Korea. On the day after the invasion, South Korea's President Syngman Rhee urgently requested ten F–51s equipped with bombs and rockets be delivered to Taegu for his Republic of Korea Air Force (ROKAF) pilots. The Far East Air Forces (FEAF) flew ROKAF pilots to Itazuke, Japan, where they were to ferry ten former target-towing P-51s. The FEAF formed a composite unit of American and ROKAF airmen initially designated 'Bout-One', which arrived at Taegu in South Korea on 30 July.

The Mustangs were better able to utilize what Korean airfields were available and, more importantly, could remain over targets longer than any jet could. Lt Gen. George E. Stratemeyer, commander, FEAF, authorised six of his F-80 squadrons to be converted to F-51s. As there were only enough Mustangs, all in storage in Japan, to equip only two squadrons, the USAF collected 145 Mustangs from Air National Guard units and sent them to Japan aboard the carrier USS *Boxer*. After modification work and pilot transition training, they were sent to Korea.

After VJ Day, the Royal Australian Air Force (RAAF) No. 77 squadron re-equipped with P-51Ds and deployed to Iwakuni in Japan as part of the British Commonwealth Occupation Force. The squadron was about to return to Australia when the Korean War broke out after which it joined UN forces supporting South Korea. The squadron flew its initial escort and patrol sorties from Iwakuni on 2 July, becoming the first non-American UN unit to commence operations. A 'friendly fire' incident occurred the next day, when its P-51s attacked a train full of US and South Korean troops between Suwon and Pyongtaek, inflicting many casualties. It suffered its first fatality on 7 July when its deputy commander, S/L Graham Strout, was killed during a raid on Samchok. He was the first non-American UN servicemen to die in Korea.

The 51st FS (Provisional) based at Taegu flew the first USAF F-51D Mustang combat missions in Korea on 15 July. On 3 August the 18th FBG headquarters moved from Japan to Taegu for expanded F-51 operations. Two days later Maj.

Louis J Sebille, commander, 67th FBS, dived his damaged F-51D into an enemy position. He posthumously received the first Medal of Honor awarded to a USAF pilot in Korea.

Endangered by the North Korean Army advance to Pohang, on 13 August two 35th FIG squadrons of F-51Ds moved from Yonil airfield in South Korea to Tsuiki AB, Japan. On 27 August two USAF F-51D pilots accidentally strayed into China and strafed an airstrip near Antung, mistaking it for a North Korean airstrip at Sinuiju. No. 77 Squadron supported UN troops retreating before the North Korean advance and during August it claimed thirty-five tanks, 212 other vehicles, eighteen trains, and thirteen fuel or ammunition dumps destroyed. On 9 September the unit's Commanding Officer, W/C Lou Spence, was killed when he led four Mustangs in a low-level attack on storage facilities north of Pusan in South Korea, which had been recently captured by Communist forces.

To support the Eighth Army offensive on 17 September, 5th Air Force F-51Ds flew napalm attacks, reportedly killing more than 1,200 enemy soldiers in Tabu-dong, Yongchon, and other strongholds near the Naktong River.

Three North Korean Air Force (NKAF) Yak-9 fighters attacked USAF aircraft including F-51s over north-western North Korea on 1 November. Two F-51 pilots shot down two of the enemy aircraft, scoring the first UN aerial victories since July. Later that day, six MiG-15 jets appeared for the first time in the war and fired on a flight of F-51 Mustangs in the Yalu River area, which escaped without damage.

In October the South African Air Force (SAAF) No. 2 'Flying Cheetahs' Squadron was posted to Johnson Air Base near Tokyo for F-51 Mustang conversion. It moved to K-9 airfield near Pusan where it flew as part of the US 18th FBG, flying its first operation on 19 November. It moved to K-24 near Pyongyang, which was bombed on 28 November by an NKAF Po-2 biplane, which damaged eleven F-51s on the ground.

On 5 November No. 77 Squadron provided close air support for Australian troops for the first time in the war. Their attacks and subsequent strafing runs on the retreating Chinese allowed the Australian troops to capture their objectives that were once held by the Chinese.

However, with the entry of the Chinese in mid-October came the vastly superior MiG-15 jet fighter, some of which were secretly flown in combat by Soviet pilots, that totally outclassed any piston-engined fighter operating in the theatre and left the Mustangs of UN forces highly vulnerable to air interception. On 16 November, No. 77 Squadron began moving forward with the 35th FIG to Yonpo Airfield, near Hamhung. North Korea's counter-attack, supported by Chinese forces, led to the squadron being withdrawn to K-9 on 3 December.

As the communists advanced south at the end of 1950, No. 2 Squadron withdrew to K-10 near Chinae from where it made dive-bombing and strafing attacks against ground targets in the face of heavy ground fire and MiG-15 attacks. On 5 February

1951 F-51 pilot Maj Arnold Mullins of the 67th FBS shot down an NKAF Yak-9 7 miles north of Pyongyang to score the only USAF aerial victory of the month. During Operation *Tomahawk* on 23 March, the second airborne operation of the war, and the largest in one day, involved 120 C-119s and C-46s, escorted by sixteen F-51Ds. No. 2 Squadron had been operating from K-9 since 25 March 1951 under the operational control of 35th FIG, while their normal base at K-10 was being rebuilt.

An experimental Sikorsky YH-19 helicopter operating with the USAF 3rd Air Rescue Service (ARS) while being evaluated under combat conditions picked up a downed F-51 pilot south-east of Pyongyang on 3 April, receiving small-arms fire during the mission.

No. 77 Squadron completed its last Mustang mission on 6 April and returned to Iwakuni to begin converting to Gloster Meteor F.8s. The squadron had flown 3,872 Mustang sorties.

The first indication of enemy radar-controlled anti-aircraft guns came with the loss of three out of four F-51Ds making an air-to-ground attack against a target at Sinmak on 30 April. In May two USAAF F-51D pilots shot down by ground fire were rescued by Sikorsky H-5 helicopters of the 3rd ARS, during which they sustained damage from small-arms fire.

The routine of No. 2 Squadron's interdiction missions was broken on 9 May, when 312 aircraft of the 5th Air Force and the 1st Marine Air Wing participated in Operation *Buster*, a massive raid on the 26-km Sinuiju airfield area, which was a major North Korean airbase south of the Yalu River. Apart from hitting a number of aircraft on the ground the fighter-bombers destroyed 106 buildings.

On 11 June an USAF SA-16 Albatross amphibian of the 3rd ARS made a pickup at dusk of a downed F-51D pilot from the Taedong River near Kyomipo, North Korea, while receiving fire from both sides of the river. A pioneer in aerial reconnaissance, Col Karl L. Polifka, commander, 67th Tactical Reconnaissance Wing (TRW), was shot down and killed on 1 July while flying an RF-51 near the front lines.

With USAF F-51 units being re-equipped with jet fighters, the 39th FS were attached to the 18th FBW to centralise the Fifth Air Force's remaining Mustang assets. On 29 August ROKAF and 18th FBW Mustangs took part in three highly successful attacks on Pyongyang.

The 18th FBW, which included No. 2 Squadron, began to convert from Mustangs to F-86F at K-55 Osan-ni airfield in January 1953. The 45th TRS flew its last RF-51D mission in February, thus ending the use of USAF single-engine, propeller-driven aircraft in offensive combat in the Korean War. USAF Mustang units had lost 194 aircraft, ten to enemy fighters and the rest to ground fire. F-51Ds accounted for twelve air-to-air kills, six Yak-9s, three Il-10s, two Yak-3s and an La-7.

The SAAF's No 2 'Flying Cheetahs' Squadron had flown 10,373 Mustang sorties in Korea, lost seventy-four of its F-51s, and thirty-four of its pilots.

F-51s being loaded on the aircraft carrier USS *Boxer* at NAS Alameda, California, in July 1950 prior to being shipped to Japan. (USN)

F-51D 44-74941 *Buckeye Blitz IV* of the 36th FBS, 8th FBG, flown by Capt J. W. Rogers, was written off at K-14 Kimpo in December 1950. (USAF)

F-51D 44-73000 of the 67th FBS, 18th FBG, at Chinhae in 1950, was transferred to the ROKAF in April 1953. (USAF)

Above: 18th FBG
F-51 Mustangs at
K-10 Chinhae Airfield in
South Korea in 1951. In
the foreground is 12th
FBS F-51K-15-NT 44-12943
(USAF).

Right: P-51D
44-72427 *Sexy Sally II*
of the 39th FIS, 18th
FBG, dropping napalm
bombs on North Korea
on 1 January 1951, was
shot down by a MiG-15 in
September 1951. (USAF)

F-51D 44-74488 of the
36th FBS, 8th FBG, being
armed with 5-inch rockets
nicknamed 'Holy Moses' at
K-14 Kimpo, was written
off in July 1951. (USAF)

F-51K 45-11742 *Ol Nadsob* 67th FBS, 18th FBG, armed with 5-inch rockets taxiing through a waterlogged Chinhae in September 1951. (USAF)

RF-51D-25-NT 44-84853 *Oh-Kaye Baby*, of the 45th TRS, 67th TRW, at Kimpo in 1952. This aircraft was flown by 100-mission veteran 2/Lt Dell C. Toedt. (USAF)

RF-51D 44-84837 *Little Lynn* of the 45th TRS, 67th TRW, at Kimpo in June 1952. (USAF)

USAF F-51D 45-11736 *My Ass is Dragon* of the 12th FBS at Pusan in 1952. Maj. James Glessner had shot down a North Korean Yak-9 in this aircraft on 2 November 1950. (USAF)

Right: RF-51D 44-84778 *My Mina* of the 45th TFS, 67th TRW, at K-2 Taegu, was written off in October 1953. (USAF)

Below: A 45th TFS, 67th TRW, pilot of RF-51D 44-84775 prepares to depart from Taegu on a recce mission over North Korea. (USAF)

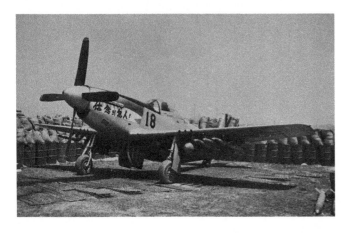

F-51D 44-74692 was assigned to Bout One on October 1950, a composite unit of American and ROKAF pilots, flown by its CO, Col. Dean Hess. (USAF)

Left: W/C Louis Thomas Spence, CO of No. 77 Squadron RAAF, was killed during an attack on North Korea on 9 September 1950 flying P-51D A68-809. (USAF)

Below: RAAF P-51Ds of No. 77 Squadron RAAF undergoing maintenance at Iwakuni Airfield in Japan in 1950. (USAF)

RAAF ground crew servicing a
No. 77 Squadron P-51D at Iwakuni in
February 1951. (UN)

A No. 77 Squadron RAAF
P-51D armed with six
5-inch-high velocity aircraft
rockets (HVAR). (RAAF)

A No. 77 Squadron RAAF
P-51D pilot returns from a
mission over North Korea in
February 1951. (UN)

No. 77 Squadron
completed its last
Mustang mission
on 6 April 1951 and
returned to Iwakuni
the next day to begin
converting to the
Gloster Meteor F.8.
(RAAF)

F-51D Mustangs
of No. 2 'Flying
Cheetahs'
Squadron, SAAF,
at K-10 Chinhae in
the winter of 1950.
(USAF)

Ground crew arm
No. 2 Squadron
SAAF F-15D 361
Miss Marunduchi with
four 5-inch forward
firing aircraft rockets
(FFAR) and napalm.
(NA)

SAAF F-51D *Miss Marunduchi* armed with FFARs and 500-lb bombs lines up to take-off from K-10 Chinhae, where it was written off landing in November 1952. (NA)

Rocket-armed No. 2 Squadron SAAF F-51D 305, preparing for a mission over North Korea, was lost in April 1951. (UN)

P-51Ds of No. 2 Squadron SAAF flew their first mission in Korea on 19 November 1950 and their last in April 1953. (USAF)

CHAPTER SEVEN

Post-war North America

Air National Guard

In May 1946 the US Government established the Air National Guard (ANG), a reserve air force manned by part-time personnel. Standards set for the ANG were those of the regular air force: service was paid and from four to ten hours training monthly was required during three years of enlistment from the eighteen to fifty-five years age group for most ground trades, and for flying duty by younger men. Up to 1948 a total of twenty-eight ANG fighter squadrons received 700 surplus P-51s. These were redesignated F-51 when the United States Air Force (USAF) was formed in July 1947.

As the Cold War became a reality, a comprehensive plan for American air defence was approved calling for additional fighter forces. To increase USAF strength, aircraft in storage were activated including more than 200 F-51s, mainly for ANG units within Air Defense Command. The ANG F-51Ds, later joined by four squadrons of RF-51Ds, remained in service until they were gradually replaced or supplemented by F-51Hs relinquished by regular USAF units. By 1952, sixty-eight of the ninety-eight ANG squadrons were equipped with Mustangs, but within the next five years they had all been replaced by jet fighter aircraft and retired from first-line USAF service. The last propeller-driven fighter aircraft to serve in the USAF was a West Virginia ANG F-51D that was flown to the Wright-Patterson AFB on 27 January 1957.

Canada's Auxiliaries

The RAF supplied five RCAF squadrons with Mustangs during the Second World War, which operated from England, France and Italy until the they were disbanded in May 1945.

After the war, thirty USAAF surplus P-51D Mustangs were delivered to Canada in 1947, at a cost of US $10,000 each. Later deliveries of aircraft from the order for 100 additional Mustangs came from Texas Engineering Co. (TEMCO). They served in two regular Royal Canadian Air Force (RCAF) squadrons, No. 416 'Lynx' and No. 417 'City of Windsor'. The RCAF's peacetime establishment called for auxiliary squadrons and authority was granted on 15 April 1946 to form six P-51 Mustang squadrons: No. 402 'City of Winnipeg', No. 403 'City of Calgary', No. 420 'City of London', No. 424 'City Hamilton', No. 442 City of Vancouver' and No. 443 'City of New Westminster'.

By the mid-1950s, the Auxiliary began flying the Canadair CL-13A Sabre 5 jet and eighty-eight Mustangs were declared obsolete in November 1956, but a number served for target towing duties into the early 1960s.

NACA Flight Testing

Mustangs played a major part in the development of the next generation of jet fighters. It was of particular interest to aerodynamicists at the National Advisory Committee for Aeronautics (NACA) Ames Aeronautical Laboratory, NAS Moffett Field, California, that data be acquired from an aircraft in flight to use in validating wind tunnel measurements of drag in 1946. The first aircraft used in this effort was P-51B Mustang 41-7632. To carry out this experiment without interference from the propeller slipstream, the propeller of the aircraft was removed and its oil and coolant ducts blocked so that it resembled the wind tunnel model. The aircraft was towed aloft by a P-61 and released. Careful measurements of longitudinal deceleration were used to determine aircraft drag, and the pilot of the Mustang made a powerless, gliding landing.

High-speed buffet was evaluated in dive tests with a P-51B during which the pilot observed sunlight refracting through the shock wave, identifying its presence on the wing and noting a correlation between its movement and the occurrence of buffeting. One P-51B, one P-51D, and two P-51H Mustangs were the primary aircraft used at Ames in wing-flow test flights.

Used for supersonic airflow tests, mini airfoil models with sensors were placed on top of the P-51's wing near the gun bays, with equipment to record the telemetry installed behind the pilot. Tests usually started from 30,000 feet when the P-51 was put into a 25–30 degree dive to achieve a max Mach number 0.732, which was enough to make the airflow over the wing reach supersonic speeds. Tests data help designers with models like the F-86 Sabre and Bell X-1.

F-51D NACA 148 was transferred to the NACA High-Speed Flight Research Station (HSFRS), at Edwards, California, from the Langley Aeronautical Laboratory, Hampton, Virginia, in 1950. This aircraft had been used in laminar-flow research at Langley prior to its transfer. The aircraft was also used as a chase and support aircraft 395 times. Neil Armstrong was among the pilots using it to chase some of the experimental X-planes before it was retired in 1959 as the result of a taxiing mishap.

NACA used fifteen test Mustangs including P-51Bs, P-51Ds, P-51Hs and one of the three experimental lightweight XP-51Fs, which were all heavily instrumented for flying qualities evaluations and stability and control measurements.

Racers and Record Breakers

Two Mustangs became prolific post-war record breakers and race winners. On 31 August 1946, Jacqueline Cochran, the former director of the wartime Women Airforce Service Pilots (WASP), flew her P-51B NX28388 *Lucky Strike Green* in the 2.048-mile Bendix Trophy Race from Metropolitan Airport, Van Nuys, California, to Cleveland Municipal Airport. She finished in second place behind Paul Mantz, who won the 2,045-mile race at 435.5 mph in his P-51C NX1202 named *Blaze of Noon*.

Mantz also won the 1947 Bendix Trophy Race at 460 mph and that same year, he used his Mustang to set coast-to-coast speed records going in both directions. On 10 December 1947 near the Santa Rosa Summit in the Coachella Valley of south-eastern California, Jacqueline Cochran flew NX28388 over a 100-km closed circuit, averaging 469.549 mph. She set both a US National and a Fédération Aéronautique Internationale (FAI) World Records that still stand. On 22 May 1948, Jackie set another world and national record of 447.470 mph over a 2,000-km closed circuit from Palm Springs to Flagstaff, Arizona, and return. Two days later she set another world and national record of 431.094 mph over a 1,000-km closed circuit from Palm Springs to Flagstaff, Arizona, and return.

Mantz won the 1948 Bendix Trophy Race at 446.11 mph ahead of Linton Carney's P-51D and Jackie Cochrane's P-51C. After the race, Jackie asked another pilot, Lockheed test pilot Sampson Held, to ferry the *Lucky Strike Green* back to California from Cleveland, but NX28388 crashed 6 miles south of Sayre, Oklahoma, on 8 September 1948, killing Held.

In 1949, Anson Johnson won the Thompson Trophy that preceded the Bendix Trophy Race with his ex-USAF P-51D, N13Y, which was one of the first of its type to appear on the US civil register, at a speed of 383.767 mph. During the race, Bill Odom, racing Jackie Cochran's highly modified P-51 *Beguine*, crashed into a house killing himself and two occupants. However, the fourth, and last, Bendix Trophy Race went ahead in 1949 and was won by a P-51C named *Thunderbird* owned by film actor Jimmy Stewart and flown by Joe DeBona at a speed of 470 mph. Mantz's NX1202 with 'Fish' Salmon in the cockpit, and renamed *The Houstonian*, took third place.

Paul Mantz had sold NX12012 to Pan American World Airways Captain Charles F. Blair, Jr., who flew the P-51C, now named *Excalibur III* on 31 January 1951 from New York International to London Airport in 7 hours 48 minutes, with an average speed of 446 mph. Blair flew *Excalibur III* from Bardufoss, Norway, to Fairbanks, Alaska, via the North Pole on 29 May 1951. He flew the 3,260 miles non-stop in 10 hours 27 minutes.

Having lost her first two Mustangs in tragic accidents, on 19 December 1949 Jackie Cochran bought another P-51C, Jimmy Stewart's *Thunderbird*, for US $1.00. The next day she flew her new airplane to two FAI World Records for Speed Over a 500-kilometer Closed Circuit Without Payload, and a US National Aeronautic Association record, with an average speed of 436.995 mph. Jackie set yet another FAI record on 9 April 1951, flying NX5528N to an average speed of 464.374 mph over a straight 9.942-mile course at Indio, California. Jackie Cochran had owned *Thunderbird* for just over three years when, on 20 January 1953, she sold it back to Jimmy Stewart for 'US$1.00 and other consideration'. He later sold it to Joe DeDona.

On the other side of the world, a series of less successful attempts to break records with a P-51 had begun. In April 1962, the pilot of a former RAAF Mustang Mk 21 was planning another long-distance record. The pilot was a Scottish Grand Prix and Le Mans winning racing car driver Ron Flockhart, who was about to fly to Bankstown near Sydney prior to the record attempt. Using the Mustang registered G-ARUK, he intended to break the Australia to England speed record for a single engine aircraft. Soon after taking off from Moorabbin Airport in Melbourne, he flew into clouds, crashed into the Dandenong Ranges and was killed.

Ron Flockhart had previously attempted the record in another former RAAF Mustang, a Mk 20 registered G-ARKD, which had been abandoned at Athens in March 1961 after the Merlin engine overheated in the hot weather.

P-51D 44-15240 was assigned to the 336th Combat Crew Training Squadron at Sarasota, Florida, in 1945. (USAF)

Above: F-6D Mustangs of the 363rd Tactical Reconnaissance Group at Shaw Field, South Carolina, in November 1946. (USAF)

Left: F-51D-25-NA 44-73348 was delivered to the 162nd FS, 357th FG, Ohio ANG, in 1947. (USAF)

F-51Ds of the 187th FS, 153rd FG, Wyoming ANG, which were delivered in 1949. (USAF)

Above: Line-up of F-51D-25-Ns from the 192nd FBS, Nevada ANG, on the 131st FBG ramp at George AFB, Victoria, California, in August 1952. (USAF)

Right: An P-51H from the 195th FS, California ANG, was based at Van Nuys Airport, California, in 1952 as part of US Air Defense Command. (USAF)

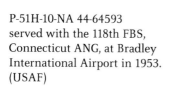

P-51H-10-NA 44-64593 served with the 118th FBS, Connecticut ANG, at Bradley International Airport in 1953. (USAF)

P-51Hs operated by the 104th FS, 53rd Fighter Wing, Maryland ANG, 'Guardian Angels' based at Harbor Field, Baltimore, until 1955. (USAF)

An F-51D, serial number of 44-74202, sits on the flight line of the Kentucky Air National Guard Base in Louisville in 1955. (Kentucky ANG)

High tail F-51D, at Spaatz Field Pennsylvania, served with the 148th FIS, 112th FG until the unit was inactivated in June 1956. (USAF)

On 27 January 1957, F-51D 0-472948, of the 167th FS, West Virginia ANG, was the final individual Mustang on duty anywhere with any American unit when it flew from Martinsburg to Wright Patterson AFB, Ohio (USAF)

RCAF Mustang Mk 4 9232, ex-USAF P-51D-30-NA 44-74502 of No. 1 Armament School, was based at Trenton, Ontario, in 1950. (James Craik)

RCAF Mustang Mk 4 9233, ex-USAF P-51D-30-NA 44-74505 of No. 1 Flying Training School, firing a 5-inch rocket, was flown secretly to Cuba in November 1958 and served with the Cuban Rebel Air Force. (RCAF)

RCAF Mustang
Mk 4 9249, ex-USAF
44-73864 of No. 420
'City of London' RCAF,
flying off London,
Ontario. (RCAF)

RCAF Mustang
Mk 4 9591, ex-USAF
P-51D-30-NA 44-74425,
serving with No. 403
'City of Calgary'
Squadron in 1957.
(Lynn Garrison)

P-51B 43-12094
assigned to NACA
Ames Aeronautical
Laboratory, NAS
Moffett Field,
California, in
November 1944 used
for laminar-flow tests.
(NASA)

NACA P-51B 43-12105 at Langley Field equipped with wing gloves for an investigation of low-drag performance in flight in 1946. (NASA)

A technician mounts a model of a P-80 aircraft on the wing of a NACA P-51D in 1948. In high-speed dives the instrumented model returns aerodynamic data on transonic flight. (NASA)

High-tailed F-51D NACA 148 was transferred to the NACA High-Speed Flight Research Station (HSFRS), at Edwards, California, from Langley in 1955. (NASA)

P-51H NACA 130 was transferred from the USAAF to NACA Ames Aeronautical Laboratory, at Moffett Field, California, and served until 1965. (NASA)

Left: Paul Mantz in the cockpit of his P-51C-10-NT, 44-10947, registered NX1202 and named *Blaze of Noon*. (NASM)

Below: Jackie Cochran's P-51B-15-NA Mustang, 43-24760, registered NX28388 and named *Lucky Strike Green*, on the flight line at the Cleveland National Air Races, 1948.

Mantz's P-51C NX1202, now named *The Houstonian*, finished second in the 1948 Bendix Trophy Race flown by Linton Carney. (NASM)

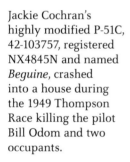

Jackie Cochran's highly modified P-51C, 42-103757, registered NX4845N and named *Beguine*, crashed into a house during the 1949 Thompson Race killing the pilot Bill Odom and two occupants.

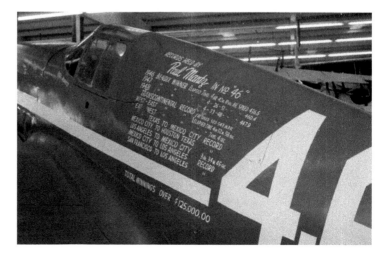

The impressive record tally on Paul Mantz's P-51C-10-NT, 44-10947, No. '46' registered NX1202. (David Oliver)

Wilson Newhall flew TP-51K Mustang, 44-12139, registered N40055 in the 1949 Cleveland National Air Races. It was sold to the Israeli Air Force in 1951. (NASM)

CA-18 Mustang Mk 22 G-ARKD flown by racing driver Ron Flockhart on his attempt to break the Australia to England record, which was abandoned in Athens in March 1961. (Geoff Goodall)

CHAPTER EIGHT

South American Operators

The Cavalier Aircraft Corporation (CAC) was originally formed in 1957 by Florida businessman David Lindsay and named Trans Florida Aviation. In 1967 the USAF placed a contract for 12 P-51D Mustangs to be remanufactured by the CAC as two-seat counter-insurgency (COIN) fighters, and two-seat trainers. They were purchased for delivery under Project Peace Condor to foreign nations through the US Military Assistance Program mainly in South America. Two two-seat Cavalier P-51Ds had also been operated from the US Army Aviation School at Fort Rucker, Alabama, to train foreign pilots in 1968.

Cavalier also developed the single-seat Mustang II as a private venture powered by a 1.750-hp Merlin 620 engine, which increased the gross weight to 13,700 lb, and fitted with 110 US-gallon tip tanks. In addition to its armament of six 0.5-inch guns it could carry six LAU-3A rocket pods.

El Salvador

One of the countries to receive Cavalier Mustangs was El Salvador. The Salvadoran Air Force (FAS) first saw action in the 1969 Football War against Honduras equipped with four Cavalier Mustang IIs. On 16 July, two of them prepared for a mission to attack Puerto Cortez. Unfortunately, they collided in the darkness near the end of runway 33 at Ilopango, causing minor damage and the mission to be aborted. Both were flown by American mercenaries.

On 17 July two Honduran Air Force Corsairs engaged two Salvadoran Cavalier Mustang IIs, attacking another Corsair while it was strafing targets south of Tegucigalpa. One of the Mustangs was shot down and its pilot was killed when his parachute failed to deploy. The Football War was the last conflict in which piston-engined fighters fought each other. An undetermined number of P-51Ds were illegally purchased by El Salvador after the conflict, which were operated during late 1970s against isolated guerrilla actions that rapidly developed into a civil war. The last FAS Mustang was sold in 1975.

Costa Rica

In 1955, the Organization of American States authorised the procurement of four F-51D airplanes for use by the government of Costa Rica to counter an invasion of Nicaraguan-backed rebels. These were procured on 16 January 1955 for US $5,500 each from the US Government and were formerly attached to the 182nd Fighter Squadron of the Texas Air National Guard. Since Costa Rica had no air force, they were operated by freelance Costa Rican Government pilots from 1955 until 1964.

Cuba

Michel Yabor was a Cuban Rebel Air Force (FAR) pilot who was able to purchase a surplus USAF F-51D from Leeward Aeronautical Sales in Miami in April 1958. A second Mustang, an ex-Royal Canadian Air Force P-51D, was also sold on the US civilian market where it was bought by an Allen McDonald, presumably a cover name for an FAR operative. The aircraft were secretly flown out of the US on 23 November by Michel Yabor and Adolfo Diaz Vazquez to Mayari Arriba in Cuba where they suffered minor damage from friendly fire from the rebels.

Following the rebel victory, the two Mustangs were transferred to Columbia airfield in Havana. They saw combat again when, on 15 April 1961, aerial attacks preceded the Bay of Pigs invasion. During these attacks, both Mustangs were damaged but only one could be repaired by 20 April, at which time the fighting was already over. The two Mustangs remained in active FAR service until June 1961 when the first Soviet-supplied MiG-15bis were delivered to Cuba.

Nicaragua

In 1947, Nicaragua purchased a small number of P-51Ds. The Nicaraguan Air Force (FAN) then received twenty-six P-51D Mustangs and spare parts from Sweden in January 1955, for a reported cost of US $650,000, to form a fighter squadron.

According to a US intelligence document dated 1 January 1955, 'President Somoza has stated that he desires to keep only five or ten of the aircraft and that he will sell the remainder.'

In August 1958, a registered agent of the Dominican Republic arrived in Managua with a letter of credit for US $139,500 to purchase from six to twelve FAN P-51s, plus spares, for the government of Indonesia but it was unclear whether or not this sale was ever completed.

Later, the US delivered another seven aircraft and two TF-51Ds and as of 31 August 1959 the FAN inventory stood at fourteen P-51s bought in Sweden, one TF-51D and seven F-51Ds bought from the USAF in 1958, although it was reported that only 50 per cent of them were in regular use. The TF-51 was sold to Trans Florida Aviation in July 1959 and nine surviving Mustangs were sold to the US Maco Sales Financial Corp in September 1965. Three FAN P-51s had been lent to anti-Castro Cuban exiles for use during the Bay of Pigs operation in 1961 but were never used. It is also possible that FAN Mustangs were used in 1980 by Sandinista rebels.

Guatemala

A CIA unit was formed in 1954 with two F-51Ds received from the Texas ANG. The aircraft were used extensively during Operation *SBSuccess* to overthrow the Guatemalan President Jacobo Arbenz, who had been deemed a Communist and a dangerous influence in Central America. The CIA F-51s, which were the first to be used in Central America, operated from Las Flores to support rebel exiles.

After the end of hostilities, an agreement was made to unite the national air force with the CIA's 'Liberation' air force into a new Guatemalan Air Force (FAG). In exchange, it received a P-51D from Sweden. On 15 January 1955, during a border dispute with Costa Rica, an FAG P-47 shot down an opposing F-51D Mustang. In 1965, the FAG's 3rd Squadron was based at Ciudad de Guatemala equipped with F-51Ds, which were used against leftist insurgents.

At the beginning of the 1970s, there was also tension concerning a dispute with the UK over the territorial status of neighboring British Honduras, now Belize. In 1971 the FAG forward-deployed seven F-51s to an airstrip at Tikal, near the border. When the British reinforced its garrison the diplomatic tension eased and conflict was averted.

At least thirty P-51Ds had been acquired from various sources including Israel, some of which had been upgraded by Trans Florida Aviation in Florida, and equipped four FAG composite squadrons until 1972. The Mustang was also flown by the FAG aerobatic teams, the 'Cofres' and the 'Machitos'.

Uruguay

In 1950, twenty-five F-51D Mustangs were sold by the US to the Uruguayan Air Force (FAU) and were used to form its No. 2 Fighter Group. They were used as fighter bombers until 1960, when they were replaced by F-80C jet aircraft, the surviving aircraft being sold to Bolivia for a dollar apiece.

Bolivia

In July 1954, the Bolivian Air Force (FAB) received two F-51Ds and one TF-51D. One was lost during the ferrying and was later replaced. In the following years, under the US Military Assistance Program to fight against pro-communist guerrillas, more Mustangs were delivered. These included eight F-51Ds that had previously served in Uruguay, which were delivered in 1960, and nine Cavalier Mustang IIs in 1967. Bolivia received a total of twenty-five Mustangs which it used in a single squadron until 1978 when they were replaced by T-33 jet aircraft.

Dominica

The Dominican Republic Air Force (FAD) received eighteen Mustangs in September 1948, a mix of P-51B, C and Ds which were flown by Brazilians mercenaries who trained the local pilots. The FAD received forty-two additional surplus P-51Ds from Sweden in 1952. Twenty-seven of them were modernised by the Cavalier Aircraft Corporation and used during the 1965 civil war, while others were acquired via the US Peace Hawk program.

When civil strife broke out in the Dominican Republic in April 1965, the United States launched Operation *Power Pack* during which the last Mustang ever to be downed in combat was shot down by a US forces.

When the FAD's DH Vampire jet fighters were retired and not replaced by Hawker Hunters as planned, the Mustangs remained the sole Dominican frontline fighters. The final FAD combat operation took place in 1983 when a Cuban intelligence ship refused to leave Dominican waters and the Mustangs strafed it. The last FAD P-51s flew until 1984, making them the world's last operational Mustangs.

P-51D-20-NA, ex-44-72086, was delivered to the Royal Swedish Air Force in 1945 and sold to the Dominican Republic Air Force, serial FAD 1936, in 1953.

P-51Ds FAD 1912 and FAD 1916. Dominica was the last military operator of the Mustang, which flew them until 1984. (Col Bonilla)

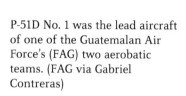

P-51D No. 1 was the lead aircraft of one of the Guatemalan Air Force's (FAG) two aerobatic teams. (FAG via Gabriel Contreras)

FAG P-51D 315, ex-44-74902, loaded with drop tanks and 5-inch rockets, was one of the last Mustangs to operate in Guatemala before being sold in the US in 1974. (FAG via Gabriel Contreras)

Ground crew re-arming P-51D FAG 336's six 0.5-inch Colt-Browning machine guns. (FAG via Gabriel Contreras)

CHAPTER NINE

Turbine Mustangs

In 1968, Cavalier Aircraft Corporation owner-founder David Lindsay, who has acquired the design rights of the P-51, began developing a highly modified version of the Mustang for use as a COIN aircraft. The Turbo Mustang III was a P-51D powered by a 1,740-shp Rolls-Royce Dart turboprop driving a four-bladed Dowty-Rotol propeller and was the ultimate development of the original Second World War North American P-51 Mustang. Making its first flight in December 1967, the single prototype Mustang III had a maximum speed of 541 mph and could carry a weapons payload of 4,000 lb on six underwing hardpoints. It was demonstrated to the USAF Tactical Air Command at Langley AFB as a potential interim AX tactical fighter but no production contract was forthcoming.

Seeking a company with mass production capability, the Turbo Mustang III, renamed the Enforcer, was sold to Piper Aircraft Corp in late 1970. In 1971, Piper built two Enforcers by heavily modifying two existing Mustang airframes, fitting them with Lycoming YT55-L-9A turboprop engines along with numerous other significant modifications. One airframe was a single-seat aircraft designated the PE-1 and the other a dual-control aircraft designated the PE-2. Prior to the Pave COIN evaluation, PE-2 was lost in a crash off the Florida coast on 12 July 1971 due to flutter caused by a Piper-modified elevator trim tab. Although the Enforcer PE-1 performed well in the 1971–1972 Pave COIN test flown by USAF pilots, Piper failed to secure a USAF contract.

In 1984 with a US $12 million appropriation from Congress, Piper built two new Enforcer prototypes designated PA-48s. The first prototype Enforcer, a former Nicaraguan Air Force P-51D powered by a 2,445-shp Avco Lycoming T55-L-9 turboprop, flew from Lakeland, Florida, on 9 April 1983. The PA-48s were tested during 1983 and 1984 at Eglin Air Force Base, Florida, and Edwards Air Force Base, California. As in the Pave COIN tests of 1971, the PA-48s were found to perform well in their intended role, but the USAF decided not to purchase the aircraft.

The Enforcer was not the only turboprop conversion of the Mustang. CA-18 Mustang Mk 22 A68-187, built in 1950, was withdrawn from RAAF service in 1957 and sold to a succession of civil owners. It was Purchased by F. Horace 'Hockey' Treloar from Sydney in 1969, who was a land developer and aviation enthusiast. Treloar engaged Aerostructures Pty, an airframe modification specialist business located at Bankstown Airport, to design and carry out the re-engining of A68-187 with a Rolls Royce Dart 510 turbine engine reportedly acquired from Trans-Australia Airlines Vickers Viscount spares stock.

In 1971 work commenced at Bankstown and the Dart turbine engine installed. Aerostructures Pty Ltd relocated to Canberra Airport in 1972 and the partially modified Mustang was moved by road to Canberra where work continued on the modification to the turbine Mustang, which was completed in 1974. Modifications included the removal of ventral radiator and oil cooler scoop, complete recowling of the engine forward of the firewall, a new electrical system and cockpit instrumentation, and the installation of two 110-gallon CAC Sabre drop tanks. Airframe streamlining and weight reduction reduced the weight by 660 kg. Ground runs were completed but the aircraft was never flown.

It remained stored at Canberra Airport until 1983 when Treloar intended to have it restored back to its original configuration with a Merlin engine. He eventually sold it to an American company, which rebuilt it as a two-seat Merlin-powered TP-51D at Chino, California, in 1996. It currently flies in USAF markings registered N50FS.

The P-51 was born to the powered by the Rolls-Royce Merlin and the fact that more than 180 Mustangs powered by that engine remain airworthy in 2023 proves it was the perfect combination for such an iconic aircraft.

The single Cavalier Turbo Mustang III, a P-51D powered by a 1,740-shp Rolls-Royce Dart turboprop, flew in December 1967.

The Piper Aircraft Corp built two Enforcers, heavily modified Mustang airframes fitted with Lycoming YT55-L-9A turboprops. (Piper)

Aerostructures Pty modified a former RAAF CA-18 Mustang Mk 22 with a Rolls Royce Dart 510 turbine in 1974, but it never flew. (Geoff Goodall)